Listen! You Can Hear Them!
The Voices of Our Ancestors!

By Jeffrey Andrew Fadiman, M.A., Ph.D. Dip. Ed. (British)

To Titus Mbui Murithi~
Whose love for the Meru past has inspired my own. My deepest
thanks for accepting me, as an elder, into your Meru family.

To Kiraitu Murungi~
Former Minister of Kenya, Former Governor of Meru, always
one who loves the Meru past. My deepest thanks for accepting
me, as an elder, into the Meru nation. It is my greatest honor.

To Gituuru wa Gikamata (cover), believed to be the oldest
man in Meru when I arrived in 1969. My deepest thanks for
acccepting me as a younger Mumeru, and therefore teaching me
so many stories about the Meru past.

My deepest thanks to Laura Lee Huttenbach, for having written
a Meru historical classic: "The Boy Has Gone: Conversations
with a Mau Mau General." Her writing has inspired mine.

Chapter 15 | The Golden Years

Chapter 16 | Muchunku, There are More Stories to Hear!

Reference

Map of Kenya showing the 47 counties. The Ameru occupy two counties, Meru and Tharaka-Nithi.

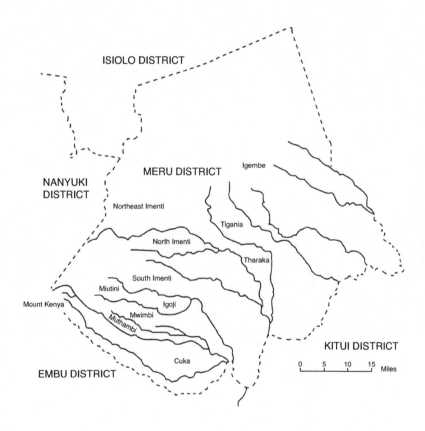

Meru: Major subgroups, 1906 (The moment of conquest)

Introduction I

To the Young Men and Women of Meru: A Greeting

"Muuga, nthaka na aari ba Meru. Riri ni iukuu rienu."

Greetings, young men and women of Meru. This is your book. This is your story. This is your history.

You have just graduated (or are near graduation), from a secondary school or university. You have worked long and hard to learn to read entire books in English. You have succeeded. You also know something of Europe's history, and perhaps that of East Africa. Indeed, you had to know *something* in order to pass the school examinations that the Europeans themselves had written.

How much, however, do you know of your own history—of Meru history? Would you like to know more? What do the words *Mbwa, Nguo Ntune, Mugiro, Aathi, Kagita, Kangangi, Kivunja,* and *Mau Mau* mean to you? They mean nothing to anyone who is not Meru. However, each word should make you think of a time in "our" history, when the Meru were struggling to overcome enemies and become the increasingly respected nation they are today.

Did I just write "our" history? Yes. I am *Muchunku* (a White man), but also *Mumeru.* I am Professor Jeff Fadiman. Fifty years ago, when I was young, I came to Meru to learn what was then known as the wisdom of elders.

Today, you and I might call it the Ameru traditional history. Fifty years ago, however, it had disappeared, crushed by the contempt of colonialists who taught the children of that time that the stories Meru grandfathers told around the nightly fires were either false, fiction, witchcraft, anti-Christian or simply not worth learning. "History," they told you, "comes from books."

"Europeans did things in the past, then wrote them down. Since the Meru did not write things down, they clearly had done nothing in the past—and therefore had no history."

All this, of course, was racist rubbish and a crime against any civilized people. Every age-set in Meru had seen and done and experienced wonderful things. Meru history is one of the richest and most exciting stories in Africa. However, all of those experiences had been locked inside the minds of the oldest living elders. To avoid the White man's hostility or contempt, they had stopped reciting them.

When I first reached Meru, however, very few of these elders—the age-sets of Kiramana, Murungi, Miriti—remained alive. Worse, they lived far from each other—scattered all over Meru, although still connected by kinfolk, friends, and reputation.

Every one of them had spent decades silently resenting those Whites who described their traditional knowledge as worthless. This was particularly true of those elders who battled to preserve the supernatural traditions—the sacred world of the ancestral spirits and those who were able to reach them by means of ritual.

The colonialists had decreed that there was no longer room in all Africa for traditional religions, and still less for practitioners of the rituals required to both contact the ancestors and implement their wishes. All this had been redefined, by the conquerors, as "African witchcraft" and was against colonial law.

In consequence, Meru elders fought back with the only weapon available to the militarily defeated—the weapon of silence. No *muchunku* (White man) was to learn anything of the *nkoma* (ancestral spirits), *urogi* (cursing), *uga* (curse removal), *uringia* (curse detection), *aroria* (ancestral prophecy), or *ugwe* (contact with ancestors).

When I came to Meru, however, the surviving Kiramana, Murungi, and Miriti elders had begun to worry about the knowledge that might be lost as they died. For these dignified old men, death posed a problem no prior set of elders had faced.

Tradition required them to pass on their "wisdom" to younger generations. However, those younger generations no longer sought them out, or visited them with the gifts required by tradition—the gourds of milk, millet beer, honey wine, meat, and snuff that not only sweetened the lives of many elders but permitted them to live out their final years in economic dignity. For every prior generation of elders, these visits had formed an informal but effective means of social security. The older one grew, the more older boys and younger men appeared, and no elder knew hunger. Now, no one came.

Instead, the younger age-sets had either been exposed to British schooling or affected by it, thus forming the first generations to believe that "wisdom" lay in books, school rooms, and the mouths of White teachers, rather than in the elders' traditions. Without exception, men of the oldest living age-sets—the last non-literate Meru—were embittered at those younger than themselves. If asked, they described the younger age-sets as having been

"Bent by the British as though they were twigs instead of men…they scratch in books like foolish guinea hens, seeking seeds (of wisdom) from White men, while ignoring their own."

How the "Lost" Traditions Were Found

When I visited these elders, I hoped to revive the tradition that younger Meru seek wisdom from the aged. I never went alone, but always accompanied by one, two, or sometimes several young men—each of whom would have been a fine warrior, had warriorhood survived. Among this group, my foreignness was unimportant. As long as I was nothing more than the oldest member of a band, Meru elders could once again feel they were teaching Meru youth.

We came with the traditional gifts: always tobacco, sometimes millet beer, once honey wine. We presented the gifts with the traditional words and gestures of respect. Then, we sat and listened and listened—sometimes for hours—until each tradition had been fully told. Only then could we ask questions.

I am now old. I have already transmitted most of the words the elders told me in a great book, meant for the oldest living generations. It is time for another book—this one for you—the young men and women of Meru. I have used the elders' teachings when I could. If I found gaps in a tradition, I filled them with what I feel they would have taught me, had I asked. I will leave it to you to guess what I have added.

Two things I do promise: If you read this book, you will have learned much Meru history. You will also have learned much history of the Meru supernatural—the rituals used to contact the *nkoma* (ancestral spirits), seek their advice, follow it, and receive their blessings.

Making contact with the supernatural has nothing to do with European ideas of witchcraft. Such accusations were made by Whites who deliberately chose to learn nothing at all about African ways of thought. European ideas of witchcraft reflected a system meant to only cause harm. In contrast, the Meru system of supernatural contact is nothing less than a complex, carefully crafted, and effective method of maintaining social peace.

One final thought—this one in the words of Gituuru wa Gikamata, the oldest man in Meru at the time I first arrived.

"I have told you all of my words. Now, put them deep into your hearts (i.e. memorize them), so that when you grow old you can pass the wisdom of Kiramana, Murungi and Miriti to the Meru yet unborn, so that they will know what it means to be truly Meru."

That, I have done. Now, I pass his final wish onto you, to pass these words to your grandchildren, the Meru yet unborn.

Introduction II
To Scholars: A Warning

This book is not a work of scholarship. I have already done that, having written an earlier, thoroughly scholarly history of the Meru. That book, originally entitled *When We Began There Were Witchmen* (1993), was republished as *Meru's Golden Age* (2012). I recommend either version to scholars seeking to learn Meru history in depth and detail.

This book, however, is for the young men and women of Meru; those who have completed (or nearly completed) their formal education without having learned a single detail of their own history. The Meru story is "rattling good;" one of the most exciting in Africa. My hope is to capture that excitement on paper, so that it glows within the minds of every Meru who reads it. To do that, however, I have had to make certain adjustments to insure clarity.

Singular/Plurals

Bantu speaking peoples (the Meru among them) change the initial letters of a word to form plurals:

— One warrior: *Muthaka*. Many warriors: *Nthaka*.

— One elder's council: *Kiama*. Many of them: *Biama*.

To enhance understanding, I have used the singular form of a Meru word and added the English plural:

— One *Kiama*. Two *Kiamas*.

Quotations/Footnotes

In my scholarly books, every quotation had a source—either from written materials or the individual elder who stated it. In this book, the quotations are used to provide flavor to the historical flow, thereby intensifying reader interest. I do not believe that younger readers will care which elder said what, or which book the words came from. Each quote, however, is completely accurate. I have either spoken personally with every elder, Black and White, whom I have quoted, or have read what they have written in their books.

Gituuru Gikama, the ancestor with whom I open the book, is—obviously—fiction. I created a fictional name from that of Gituru wa Gikamata, perhaps the oldest of the many gentle Meru elders with whom I have spoken. His stories will live forever in my mind; by creating a fictional character from the memories I hold, I can hear and enjoy them once more.

Historical Dates

Most young people in my country soon learn to describe history as boring. They learn it from older children when they are young. I have seen my own four children follow the same path, learning never to express enthusiasm for the American past, lest they be condemned by their peers. However, if I ask them what they dislike so much, they answer "dates." Most young people don't mind learning *what* happened back then, but see no point in learning *when*.

This book is for young people. They know, of course, that the early Meru marked time according to age-sets—*that* event occurred in the time of *this* age-set. However, I doubt that many of today's younger Meru care about which event happened during which age-set. Most, I suspect, just want to know what happened. In consequence, I use few dates throughout the book, focusing on what happened, rather than when.

Voice

I had hoped to write the entire Meru story in the voice of Gituuru wa Gikamata, one of Meru's "old, old men." When I reached Meru to conduct my research (1969), he was universally believed to be the tribe's oldest man.

In KiMeru (the Meru language), the phrase "old, old man" does not imply someone in decline, but someone rich in wisdom. Gituuru was rich in tales of the past, told to him by his grandfather, who had learned them from his grandfather, and so on, back until the tribe's beginning.

Nonetheless, I could not tell the entire story solely in his voice. He simply did not know key portions of it. Meru history consists not only of events that happened to Meru, but the outside forces that triggered these happenings.

No elder, regardless of his wisdom, could know the colonialist plans of the British, Italians, and White Kenyans who invaded Meru society and massively reshaped its history. No elder, regardless of his wisdom, could know European thinking, whether about breech-loading rifles, luring children into schools, or their own superstitions about witchcraft. As a result, to tell the entire story, I have had reshape most, but not all, of his thoughts into my words. His words are in *bold italics*. Perhaps, we are all a bit poorer for it.

Chapter 1

Meru: In Search of "Lost" History

When I was young, impossibly handsome, and in need of a career, I was trained as an African Oral Historian. In those days, in my country, most Whites did not believe Africans had a history. My professors disagreed, but felt that it was locked inside the memories of Africa's oldest men—who had learned it from their grandfathers, who had learned it from theirs. As each aged elder died, what he knew would die too, and thus be lost to mankind. Of course, they were dying daily throughout Africa. The professors' goal, therefore, was to teach us—their new graduate students— how to locate and interview these elders—all over Africa—then record what they knew while they still lived.

In a low-key, non-dramatic way, we were taught that we were entering into a race against death. If we allowed every African elder to die before we reached them, the history of the entire African continent would be lost to mankind. Since we had only 22 students in our graduate class, and Africa held millions of elders, we were all suitably impressed and thoroughly intimidated.

Culture shock: Welcome to Meru

I chose the Meru, a tribe on Mt. Kenya. I knew nothing of them, except that they had a reputation for witchcraft. My professor suggested I learn their witchcraft along with their traditional history, recording both at once. That sounded intimidating too. I knew nothing whatsoever about African witchcraft, Meru history, or, indeed, anything about the Meru.

Thus, I timidly entered Meru to discover their past, dragging a reluctant wife, child, and toddler. Our first days with the Meru were not inspiring. Italian Catholic Missionaries had given us a house—complete with doors, windows, locks, and 400 neighbors. Ten yards away lay a huge, vibrant, noisy primary school, filled to overflowing with 400 joyous, enthusiastic, LOUD children.

Worse, not one of these children had ever seen a small White boy before, let alone a toddling White baby. Nor had any one of them ever seen a commercially produced toy. My sons had lots of toys, which they soon laid out in our front yard, as is American custom. Result: 400 children encircled the yard whenever they were not in school, cheerful, chatting, watching my children, watching the toys, and watching my children play with the toys.

No one stole a toy—ever. No one spoke to my sons, since no Meru child knew Italian—the language of the Catholic priests and every other white person they had seen. Nor did my sons. Thus, at first, my kids played in silence, which the Meru children filled with staring, comments, laughter, and general feelings of appreciation.

Somewhat over-protective, we adults decided to build a fence around the entire house. With a *panga* (long bush knife) in hand, my wife and I marched boldly into the adjacent rainforest to find and cut down whole groves of bamboo. Trees were cut and carried home by local Meru as headloads. Holes were dug, and entire lines of fresh bamboo were tidily inserted. A fence was born. Tired, we ate and slept, while ecological disaster struck the fence in little nibbles.

We woke at dawn to find that every bamboo fence pole had been carefully covered with mud. Beneath the mud lay uncountable masses of termites. Protected from the sun by the darkness of the mud, they were peacefully eating the entire row of fence poles down to the ground. Bravely, my four-year-old son and I attacked the mud with *pangas*, knocking it off and destroying their cover. Our efforts were useless. In daylight, the termites ran and hid—causing my son much pleasure. At night, however, their legions returned, the mud returned, the nibbling returned, and the fence was doomed.

My wife and I were equally disillusioned by the local market. These days what was a village has expanded and evolved into an overcrowded, busy, thriving semi-slum, within which everybody—man, woman, and child—hustles every moment of the day to sell anything to anybody at any moment.

In those days, however, the market was a semi-empty square. Along the edges, women sat on blankets and sold piles of beans—just beans. Behind them, men stood in tiny groups holding goats—just goats. In one corner, a woman offered live chickens—just chickens. My wife, who had come with her shopping bag, expecting to shop, turned to me in dismay.

"We can shell the beans, she sighed, "but what do we do with a live chicken or goat?"

"Strangle it," I muttered, wishing I was home.

Finding Meru's Eldest Elders

I was equally timid in launching my research. I had come 4,000 miles to interview elders, but had no idea how to begin. Where were they? Who were they? How old was an elder? Which elders knew most? Which elders knew anything? Which elders had been important in the past? I hadn't a clue. My first panicked interview was a house painter. I stopped him because he had white hair. Not unexpectedly, he knew more about house-painting than history. Who should be next? How should I find him? Where?

Tentatively, I hired an "outside man" and an "inside man." Fabian was the outsider. His first job was to discover the oldest and wisest men in the entire tribe. His next job was to walk me to wherever they lived—and all them lived very far from Meru's only road, either far up or far down the forest-covered mountain. His last job was to sit with me for hours as I interviewed elder after elder, translating whatever was said into English sufficient for my little tape recorder to swallow whole. He called himself "The Battlefield," since every misunderstanding and mistranslation had to pass through him.

Simon was the "inside man." Since every word we spoke on "the battlefield" went into a tape recorder, Simon would spend weeks painfully translating the elders' always-rambling tall-tale-telling into rational, logical, fact-based English that we could all follow.

As the months passed we all became Meru history experts. All three of us fell in love with the dream of uncovering the hidden nuggets of their golden past. Beyond that, they both became my dearest friends, guiding my steps as I stumbled back and forth and up and down the slopes of this beautiful mountain.

I wrote a letter to my father, describing my first terrifying morning, when I realized I actually had to do this research. Who would have thought that he would keep it for 61 years? Some of it reads:

"I wake at dawn. 100 rosters have gathered outside my bedroom window to SCREAM. I hate the roosters. I hate this place. I am mucho nervous! My first day of interviewing and I don't know who to interview. How should I know which elders know what happened way back then?

"KNOCK, KNOCK! Oh God! It's barely light outside and someone's here. A Meru Catholic Priest greets me, in deep distress. 'Come! Please! Our dear old man is dying. Before the Whites came, he was our war-leader and after they ruled us, our greatest chief. Now his heart is weak. He says God is only keeping him alive so that he can speak of what he knows to you.' I grab my tape recorder.

"KNOCK, KNOCK! It's Fabian. 'Come! Please! The oldest of the oldest men in my region comes from the family of Meru prophets. When he was young, he says he was carried off by nkoma (ancestral spirits) into our sacred forest and taught by them how to see the future. Now he has many children but none want to hear what he knows. Please come and write what the nkoma taught him into books before he dies.'

"KNOCK, KNOCK! It's Simon. 'Come! Please! I found a man who once did witchcraft. When Whites came he discovered Jesus and forgot it. Now, he is near death and wants to tell you

how it was done so that his children will read what you write before he dies.'"

My first, carefully concealed thought was that I either wanted to go back to bed or go home.

Meru History from Meru Elders

We went, of course. In one long day, I spoke with the war leader, the prophet, and the witchdoctor. The stories they told me ran hours. However, their final message was the same:

"Our sons no longer come to us to learn wisdom."
"The British have taught them that wisdom is only in books."
"You write books! Now, write (my) wisdom in them."
"Then, give your books to (my) children and grandchildren yet unborn, so that they will always know what it means to be truly Meru."

I promised. Eventually, I would conduct more than 300 interviews with over 100 of the oldest Meru. That first night, however, I just lay in bed and thought about how lucky I was to meet and actually talk with a war-leader, a prophet, and a witchdoctor. Nobody did that. Most people just commute to work and deal with traffic jams. As I fell asleep, my final thought was "It's scary here, particularly with kids, but I think I will come to love Meru." And I have.

My days after that evolved into a pattern. Each dawn, the 100 roosters would gather together outside my bedroom window to SCREAM until I woke up. Each breakfast, I would develop stomach cramps from the anxiety I felt at having to walk outside, find an elder, and convince him to answer my questions. Each morning, I would gulp black Meru coffee, dissolve the cramps, smile at my watching children, and pretend I was an African History Researcher.

Then, as each sun rose, my two assistants would appear with the hot news of the day: A traditional prophet, or healer, or placer-of-curses (bad witchdoctor), or remover-of-curses (good witchdoctor), colonial chief, early missionary, Mau-Mau rebel, etc., would like to meet me, NOW! HURRY!

There was no madness in that method. When everyone is old and knows of things much older, they yearn to pass their wisdom to the young. No one came, but they grew older—and then came I.

Off we went each day, usually on foot. Off the road and into the rainforest—me following Fabian, who followed a guide, who followed the buffalo paths. Eventually, we would come to a hut surrounded by banana trees and goats. Each elder greeted us at his doorway. Each received my gift of traditional tobacco to smoke or chew. I then explained my tape recorder, recording and then replaying each elder's voice to show it was harmless.

Then my questions began, often to be met by a flood of narration, as the past sprang to life in the mind of each man as he relived his youth. Sometimes, an elder rose painfully up, danced a few steps, then taught me to do what he was narrating. Over time, I became expert with a spear, *simi* (short sword), war-club, and the tactics used against cattle-raiders. More interesting, I learned the so-called "witchcraft rituals," actually techniques that aged specialists used to contact *nkoma* and thus manipulate the minds of potential clientele.

Best of all, I learned to think a bit like a Meru. No one taught me. Indeed, no one knew they were teaching me. Nor did I know that I was being taught. Nonetheless, I slowly learned how Meru people think. I learned how they spoke and behaved in specific situations and thus how I should speak and behave. In a very limited sense, I had become just a bit Meru and just a bit African. I was very happy.

And then, one day, it was all over. My wife and my children were not happy, and longed to leave Meru forever. So, we did. I did not return for almost 60 years. Oh yes, my pile of notes became a Ph.D. thesis. That thesis became a book. I became a professor. But, my life had a gap. Stupidly, selfishly, I never sent a single copy of my research back to the Meru. In consequence, for another 50 years no one in Meru but Simon and Fabian knew that they even had a history!

50 Years Later: I am Meru

Fifty years went by without my thinking much about the Meru. Then, a few years ago, a Kenya Minister—also a Meru—came to Washington DC on business for his government. With time to spare, he went into a bookstore. By chance he picked up my book on Meru history, liked it, and decided to find me.

One day my phone rang.

"Are you the famous Professor Jeffrey Andrew Fadiman, M.A., Ph.D.?" asked a formal, female voice with an African accent.

"I'm Jeff Fadiman, but not famous," I replied.

"Oh, but you are—in Meru," the voice continued. "Are you the man who rediscovered our lost Meru traditional history? If so, our Minister, who is a Meru, would like to invite you to return to Meru. We wish to receive you into our nation as an honored Meru elder."

I went. It was quite a shock. I woke up on my first Meru morning with a whole new army of screaming roosters. However, when I staggered sleepily into a dining room, a TV crew and camera greeted me, then began to film the sheer excitement of me eating cornflakes.

I went through several ceremonies that day. The one I liked most was dancing down a small shallow hill with the minister, surrounded by two lines of singing, chanting, dancing Meru women, all of them laughing themselves silly because White men are universally known never to dance. Even the minister commented, laughing at me as we danced:

"Professor, you have White skin but inside, you have an African heart." That pleased me.

However, "inside" I seemed to have developed more than just an African heart. As I went through the ceremonies— giving talks, hearing talks, dancing—I also began to hear small voices in the back of my head. It was as if someone was playing a radio far away. The voices stayed with me all day, disappearing when I was surrounded by singing, shouting, or talking Meru, but always returning when I was briefly alone.

Frankly, I wasn't disturbed. Privately, I decided that I had gone insane but would fix the problem when I got back to the US and a therapist. Meanwhile, I would go on being busy, being honored, and having fun. Finally, the universally respected members of the Meru *njuri nceki*, the traditional ruling council of Meru elders who had guided the people for 300 years, proclaimed me an honored elder of the Meru nation. I had become the first White Meru elder in history. It was and has remained the greatest honor of my career.

Now, I Could Hear Them!

I went to sleep under a darkening cloud of worry. Alone, I could listen. When I listened, I could hear—but not quite. I did hear what I felt were human voices. I could either hear—or imagine I heard—individual Meru words. However, I speak no Meru, and thus was never sure.

I slept. I woke. It was still dark. I was not alone. Someone else was in the room! Panicked, I snapped on the light, grasping a *panga* and ready to fight. I saw nothing. Relieved, I took one breath—just one. Then, I listened. I could clearly hear them. The voices of the Meru ancestors—now our ancestors. I was now Meru. The rituals used to make me Meru seemed to have allowed the voices to come into my mind. Better, I could understand them—not through translation, but something else that I could not understand. One voice stood out:

"I know you, Muthungu (White man). You know me. I am Gituuru Gikama. I am Meru. I am dead. When you met me—so many, many years ago, you were young, with two baby sons, Elik and Byo'n. (Erik and Bjorn). I was old—the oldest living Meru elder. Now you are old and you are Meru. That is why you can hear (understand) me. NO! Do not look around for me. I can see you, but you cannot see me.

You can hear my voice because I am many voices—the many voices of nkoma, the ancestral spirits, the ancestors of Meru.

"We have assembled our voices to tell you the story of our people from the moment we began. Our story has passed from the tongues of grandfathers to the ears of grandchildren for 18 age-sets (est. 320 years). But now the young no longer listen. You can write, Muthungu. I have watched you do it when you were young. You must write our story, or it will die. You must write our story before you die. Begin!"

Chapter 2

Mbwa: We Began on an Island

"In the beginning, Muchunku, we were not called Meru. No one among us remembers our tribal name. My grandfathers may have known, but I was too young to ask. Now, I am too old to remember.

"We do know that we once called ourselves Ngaa. No one among us, even the oldest, knows what it means. We know, however, that we began on an Island. We called it Mbwa."

The island was small; you could walk across it in half a day and around it from sunrise to dark and never be tired. It was crooked, shaped like a badly grown gourd. The soil was mostly sand and dark rock (coral) where nothing grew. However, there was iron everywhere. Thus, the Ngaa had ironsmiths who made small knives, arrow tips, and spear points. This gave them iron-tipped spears, but not many. There was nothing big or dangerous to hunt.

There were, however, several springs of sweet water, and bits of good earth where they could grow short stalks of millet and small, wrinkled yams. The water also let them keep small flocks of goats, sheep, and sometimes cows. The island also gave them coconuts, bananas, mangoes, and smaller fruits.

Our main food, however, was fish. Our island had coral all around it, that kept fish near the beaches. We fished with small wooden fish hooks for small fish. Big ones crushed the hooks in their jaws and escaped. Every boy had a long, thin fish-stick, sharp-sharp at one end. We would wait, we would watch, we would throw, we would leap on the fish once it was pinned, and we would eat.

The Water was Evil

"Mbwa was surrounded by bitter water that no one could drink. This water was alive. Once each day it would gather itself, foam, and run away from the island to the shore of a Big Land (mainland). There, the water would eat grass until the end of each day. Then, with no warning, it would race back along the same path, angry, foaming, and glad to seize and eat any person or animal in its path.

"The water was evil. It gave no warning. When it would flow away to eat grass, it left steaming black mud, sharp rocks, and little pools into which our women could run to gather small sea-things to eat. Often, the children ran too, shrieking and gathering shells. When the water raced back, however, it would hiss as it came, giving both women and children the chance to race for the beach.

"Often it caught animals meaning to cross. Big things with hooves sometimes broke through the mud, delaying them enough for the water to catch and eat them as they struggled to break free. Sometimes the water even caught elephants. If they drowned, we would feast, with meat for everyone over many days. We kept and hid the tusks, expecting someday to trade."

The islanders lived by themselves and were content. They worked constantly to grow and find food, but there was always enough.

"We knew of people on the Big Land (mainland) with whom we could trade, or even seek wives. However, they all looked like us, ate what we ate, drank our beer, and spoke words we could mostly understand. None were enemies."

Nkoma: The Meru Spirit World

"We did not allow the living to exist on the island alone. We nkoma lived alongside them."

Every Ngaa knew what would happen in the moment he died. There would be pain and fear. Then it would stop. He would pass through a tunnel, moving toward a light. He would leave the tunnel to find himself in that part of the island held sacred to the ancestors. No one living could enter. He could rest.

Soon, however, there were tasks to do. Even within this sacred area, one must eat. There were fish to catch, crops to plant, goats to herd.

"The main task, however, was to watch over one's descendants. We could see and hear them; they neither saw nor heard us. This was pleasant. We took pleasure from watching those we knew and loved grow up."

Every living Meru was linked to his ancestors not only by the ties of kinship, but the rituals he constantly performed. These were specifically intended to keep the relationships alive. In consequence, every living Meru knew that his ancestors were alive, invisible to him, but always watching, ready to punish each deviation from tradition.

Mugiro: The Curse

"However, the watching could be painful. Sometimes, a living man might deliberately violate an ancestral tradition, behaving so as to create conflict with another living person. This might happen when one man took another man's woman or stole another man's goat. It might also occur accidentally, as when a man saw women bathing or giving birth. It might take place if a man saw one of us."

If this happened, the ancestors concerned would place a *mugiro* (curse, cast a spell) on the guilty person. A *mugiro* is a wish to harm. It is created by chanting—loudly and repeatedly—either by one ancestor or many. If many chant the curse is stronger. The words they chant are alive. They carry the power to harm living things. Thus, if someone violates tradition, *nkoma* (ancestral spirits) chant the wish that he must "sicken."

As a result, someone (or some living thing) close to the offender would become "unclean" (ritually impure). This ritually created uncleanness could lead to illness, accident, a bull sickening, a crop withering, or a baby refusing to be born.

It might harm the violator himself: A sexual crime might lead to pain in his penis. A theft could stiffen the fingers of the hand that stole. Someone who stopped another's breath (killed him) might find his own breath shrinking every day.

Whatever happened would be visible to others, thus ensuring that everyone near him would know he had been cursed. Consequently, all would shun him, avoiding contact. No one would talk with him, cook for him, sing with him, sleep with him. In consequence, no curse could simply be ignored. The victim would be cut off from human contact until it was removed.

Murogi: The Curser

Men on the island often cursed one another. Most often, each appealed to his own ancestors, asking them to hurl a curse on an immediate enemy. Some men in every generation could contact *nkoma* more successfully than others. When they called upon ancestors to curse an enemy, the intended victim—or someone near him—invariably met disaster. Thus, any angry man who sought to harm an enemy could come, secretly, to a man who specialized in the rituals used to ask *nkoma* to curse. Such a ritual specialist was called a *murogi* (curser, spell-caster); the rituals themselves were called *urogi* (cursing, casting spells).

Muga: Curse Remover; Murungia: Curse Detector

Other men approached their ancestors for other purposes, creating new rituals to convey their wishes. Some became *aga* (singular: *muga*), or curse removers. Since every man who fell to calamity believed that he was cursed, his first wish was to remove the curse. He could best do that by secretly approaching a curse remover, always at night, bearing traditional gifts—most often a goat.

Through ritual, a *muga* could symbolically remove the feelings of impurity (the curse) from a victim's mind, thereby both eliminating his mental anxiety and restoring him (or those near him) to physical health.

Still other men became *aringia* (singular: *muringia*), or curse detectors. Once a man's curse had been removed, his next concern was to decide who had cursed him—ancestor or another man. No victim of a curse could feel secure until he learned who caused it. Otherwise, his enemy might curse him again, thus reinforcing the conflict between them rather than resolving it.

He could best do this by approaching a curse detector who would use his own rituals to ask *nkoma* to help him detect the curser. Once this was done, the enmity between both men was still unresolved, and might even intensify as they each cursed the other. Tradition required, therefore, that such open enemies appeal to their *kiama* (council of elders) to resolve the issue. The council would then use still other rituals to reconcile their quarrel and restore community peace.

One example of such rituals was called "taste the hot iron." An iron was heated in fire. The *kiama* elders, chanting in unison, appealed to their ancestors to observe the test and resolve the hostility. Each man then licked the iron. If both tongues were equally burned, the conflict was declared resolved. If one tongue was more severely burned, that man was declared guilty, and forced to pay the "cow(s) of restitution" to the other. Thereafter, both men sat with the elders to "eat the bull of reconciliation." The acting of sharing meat together symbolized the end of their hostilities and the return of social peace.

Thus, the *mugiro* had several purposes:

— to harm an enemy

— to punish, by forcing him to visit (and pay goats to) a curse-remover

— to further punish by (indirectly) causing him to seek (and pay more goats to) a curse detector

— finally, to generate an appeal (using more goats) to both men's *kiama* asking it to ritually resolve the hostility between them.

In sum, the *mugiro* was nothing less than a magnificent, sophisticated method for maintaining social peace.

Mugwe: Voice of the Ancestors

Not every ritual specialist dealt with curses. One type contacted the *nkoma* to ask for their advice in guiding the island people along the paths laid out by tradition. The foremost of these of these was given the title of *mugwe*, the transmitter of ancestral blessings.

There could be only one mugwe, but one mugwe there must always be. Without mugwe, how could our ancestors command us?

Without the guidance of *mugwe*, it was believed that the island society would dissolve. His two tasks were to seek the *nkoma's* decisions in resolving human conflicts, then transmit their blessing to those of the living who were guided by those decisions. The *mugwe* was also believed—falsely—to foretell the future. In fact, his prophecies were those of the *nkoma*. Each *mugwe* was merely their voice.

No one remembers how transmitting the blessings of ancestors began. However, there was always a *mugwe* to transmit them. He was always the elder to whom all others appealed in times of change or crisis. At such times his blessing (and through him, that of the ancestors) was required in order for society to function. His word was tangible proof of ancestral approval of whatever decisions had been made. Nonetheless, there came a day when human conflict rose to unheard-of heights, and the "red darkness" covered the lives of every person on Mbwa. In this crisis, all men turned to *mugwe*.

Where was Mbwa?

Existing evidence suggests that Mbwa was on the western side of Manda Island, today part of the Lamu archipelago. The Ngaa are believed to have lived on that portion of the island closest to the mainland, adjacent to a channel that was periodically flooded and drained by a tidal bore.

Are the Nkoma Real?

The *nkoma* are real as long as they are very much alive within the minds of living Meru. Today, many Meru are either Christian or Moslem. Notwithstanding, underneath the non-African teachings imposed on them as children, many Meru remain aware of the obligations imposed on them by ancestors. They continue perform the rituals, either in reality or within their minds, if only because a display of respect to one's ancestors creates pride in themselves, their family, clan and people. By these standards the *nkoma* will live in the hearts and minds of the Meru forever.

Chapter 3

Nguo Ntuni: The Invaders

The red darkness that covered the lives of every Ngaa on Mbwa took the form of an invasion. One day (around 1700), a white-sailed ship appeared, landed, and spit out invaders.

"We knew them as the Nguo Ntune (Red Clothes), since they wore red cloth around their bodies, wrapping a smaller piece around their heads. They were taller and thinner than us. Their skin was brown. but glowed red in bright sun. They had black eyes, long noses, and thin, cruel lips that never smiled.

"They came well-armed. Each man carried a spear tipped with much iron, as well as an iron sword, the blade of which curved backwards. "Our young men were ready to fight them, but we had too few spears and those had tiny points. We had no swords—who had there been to fight? Were we to go against them with sharpened fishing sticks?"

Notwithstanding, the young men wanted to fight. They raced for the few spears available. Those without one seized a sharpened fishing stick. Swiftly, they made a single line, raised their weapons and crouched to charge.

"NO!"

The sound came from every elder at once, followed by a command that they drop the weapons. Every elder had decided simultaneously that he did not want to lose sons. It was better to surrender.

They surrendered. The victor's first act was to command Ngaa elders to show where they had hidden the many tusks collected from drowning elephants. Next, they forced young men to head-carry them to their boat. Thereafter, they commanded bigger boys to fish and feed them, dragging whatever was not eaten once again to the boat.

Over time, the bigger boys were forced to fish daily, catching to feed the Red Clothes rather than their own families. Women were put to work hoeing millet and gathering fruits—again to feed the boat.

"The men now herded our goats, which had become their goats— handing over a goat whenever the Red Clothes wished to feast. If one of us objected, his ankle was pierced, and a vine threaded through it, with the ends tied to a tree."

The Terrible Tasks

"We Ngaa made bad slaves. We produced food for the new masters but showed them our hatred when we could. Eventually, a few of their leaders grew angry. Gathering the island elders together, they set them a frightening task. If they failed one would be killed."

The task was simple; to drop a large round fruit into a deep well, then retrieve it without using either hands or a stick. The elders, baffled at first, sent spokesmen to Koome Njoe, their leading elder, and perhaps their *mugwe*. Using proper ritual, he spoke to the *nkoma*. Then, he sent the spokesmen back to the well with instructions to fill it with water. The fruit floated up and out. The *Nguo Ntune* were not pleased.

A second task was laid on the elders: to present their conquerors with an eight-sided cloth. Again, they turned to Koome Njoe. He offered them a corn husk, freshly peeled from its corn. It had eight sides. Again, the Red Clothes were not pleased.

A third task was then set: make a sandal from animal skin, but with fur on both sides. This time, Koome Njoe did not even speak. He rose, cut the dewlap from his cow, carved it into a sandal and gave it to the elders, with the fur of the cow on both sides.

Now the *Nguo Ntune* were deeply angry and spoke of killing this leading elder. Instead, they set out a harder task; to provide them a dog with horns. This took Koome Njoe some time. He sat in isolation, to perform the beloved rituals that called the *nkoma*. He then instructed the elders to kill a dikdik, a tiny antelope common on the island, and remove its horns. Next, they caught a dog, tied it to the ground, then cut two open wounds in its skull. As it bled, the two dikdik horns were placed in the wounds, then smeared around the edges with tree sap. The horned dog was then presented to the Red Clothes in hostile silence.

The *Nguo Ntune*, now deeply angry, commanded the Ngaa elders to perform a task that they all knew was impossible: to forge a spear so long that it would touch the clouds. Koome Njoe responded with profound sadness, for the *nkoma* had let him know his people's future and it seemed terrible. To survive, the Ngaa, all of them, must flee the island and wander he knew not where.

Mass Flight

At this moment, the elders were told that he had dreamed only of suffering. He instructed them to tell their hated tormentors that Ngaa smiths would construct the largest forge ever built; one able to send flames higher than anyone had ever seen. The Red Clothes were warned to move far, far away lest the ancestral power contained within the flames consume them all. Startled and uneasy, the invaders backed away, retreating to another edge of the island, where the adjacent seawater would protect them.

"When night fell, The Ngaa instantly set every one of their homes aflame, thus creating the largest fire ever seen. This provided the great glow in the sky that the Ngaa spokesmen had promised their now hated enemies."

Koome Njoe then told the elders his next truth. They were—everyone—to gather only what they could carry and flee the island to the Big Land. Once there, they were to flee further—so far that the Red Clothes could never find them. When asked where they were going, the *mugwe* admitted he did not know. When asked how they were to cross the bitter water, the *mugwe* again admitted he did not know.

Each clan was to carry something useful on the march: one group took yam stems, another herded goats, a third— that clan closest to the spirits—carried every object sacred to the tribe.

The Ngaa raced to the island's western edge, but the flight was stopped before it began. Whether by miscalculation or chance, the channel between Mbwaa and the mainland was so deeply underwater that no one dared cross.

"Mugwe responded that things were too desperate to rely on the sacrifice of a goat. Instead, he asked for three men willing to sacrifice themselves for the people. The first was to become a human altar, upon which a sacrifice could be performed. The second was to allow his stomach to be opened so that the Mugwe could examine his intestines, thereby learning what the nkoma advised. The third was a substitute, lest the second man lose his courage."

The sacrifice complete, Koome Njoe scattered powders on the waters that barred the people's way. The waves moved obligingly to one side, whether through tidal action, the *nkoma's* will or the *mugwe's* magic. The entire community then fled across to safety. Before dawn, the waters swiftly returned. The Red Clothes dared not cross.

Who Were the Nguo Ntune?

Existing evidence suggests that the *Nguo Ntuni* were Coastal Arabs, descendants of one of the earlier migrant groups from the Arabian Peninsula, who had formed commercial communities along the East African Coast. Descriptions of their physical appearance, clothes and weapons confirm this, as does their treatment of the Ngaa.

How Did Both Groups Communicate?

Coastal Arabs may well have spoken a variant of Swahili, but the Ngaa did not. Swahili had developed as a *lingua franca,* to be used by coastal peoples everywhere when conducting trade. The Ngaa may have exchanged goods with immediate neighbors, but never lived from trade, thus would not have spoken Swahili. It seems logical therefore to assume that invaders and invaded communicated in a 17th century variant of Ki-Amu, the language then used throughout the entire Lamu archipelago. This suggests, in turn, that the Red Clothes were from a nearby island, had learned of the tusks the Ngaa had collected, and decided to plunder them.

Were the Terrible Tasks Fictional or Real?

No one can say. However, the fact that every living Meru elder recites the same stories suggests that *something* terrible made a universal impact. That, in turn, suggests they may have actually occurred. It is not difficult to imagine a group of *Nguo Ntune,* bored by their existence on a small island, creating the first (and easiest) task simply to torment those they had conquered. When that failed to amuse them, they may have invented a harder task, then a still harder one, etc. Sadism exists in all human societies; why not among 17th century Coastal Arabs?

Why Did the Waters "Go Eat Grass?"

The behavior of the waters suggests the existence of a tidal bore, which appears when an incoming ocean tide is funneled into a narrow channel, forcing its leading edge into a swiftly moving wave. The tide draws the remaining waters behind it, creating an area of mud, stone, coral reefs, and flapping, stranded sea creatures. Tidal bores appear at the mouths of rivers. As the river flows into the sea, the bore strikes it, moving powerfully up river. Then, energy spent, it recedes, moving back to where it began.

The Mkanda channel lies between the western edge of Manda Island and the Kenya mainland. It has a tidal bore. It moves swiftly inland at times that change with the seasons. It then returns in a rush, drowning anything not able to escape. Logically, the leading Island elder of that era had spent long hours observing the bore's ebb and flow, until he had a fair idea of what it did and when. Thus, when traditions recall him casting magic powder into the waters, they moved!

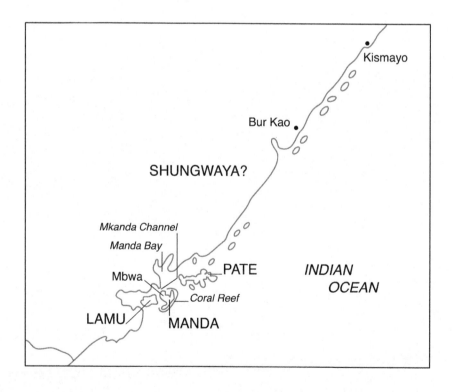

Manda Island (Mbwa): Origin of the Meru, then known as Ngaa. Manda Island is part of the Lamu Archipelago.

Chapter 4

Mass Flight to Mount Kenya

The Islanders recall taking "a long time" to cross to the mainland. Logically, moving heavily laden through darkness and mud, they worked for hours. Goat hooves would have broken through the muddy crust and mired the animals. Thus, again logically, each goat must have been hand-carried across the waterway by the men, while the women were equally burdened with baskets of yams.

Once on the far shore, they moved south and inland, heading for what they either knew or had heard of as a red sea. Evidence suggests that this was the Tana River in flood. The river begins far inland, flowing out of the Aberdare Mountains. It runs 1000 km (641 mi), to empty into the Indian Ocean near Manda. During rainy seasons the river overflows its banks, extending whole kilometers in all directions. Then, it drifts—slowly and shallowly seaward. The traditions emphasize that the fleeing migrants took a long time to cross. One can imagine the depth of their fears, wading through water, however shallow, holding their yams and herding their goats, but looking out across a water that seemed never to end. Nor could they have imagined what was on the other side.

Once across, they moved north along the river's inland bank. Spurred on by fear of recapture, the group became migrants in fact, trekking for entire seasons along the river's edge. Periodically, they came across a piece of fertile land where they could settle. The women grew small crops of millet. The boys fished the river, using the same spears and wooden fish hooks they had used before. The men not only herded the goats in daytime but guarded them at night—for there was danger.

Saving Goats: Spearing Lions

In those days, hyena, leopards, and lions were everywhere. Lions, in particular, came every night for goats. The migrants tried circling their settlements with thorn-branch fences. The lions jumped over them, ignored the guards, seized goats, then leaped the thorns once more. The migrants built the fences higher. Now the lionesses came, scrambling up and over the higher barrier, then climbing back, goat in jaws.

Nor could the young men effectively fight lions with spears. To throw a spear was useless. It would barely penetrate a swiftly moving lion. Nor was a spear thrust much better. The small spear heads pierced the intruders but could not be pushed in far enough to do real damage. Worse, a lion, once lightly speared, could turn to bat the spear away, charge, and kill.

"We found a plan. Our herd was, each night all night, guarded by three men, each with an iron-tipped spear. When a lion leaped the barrier to seize a goat, all three spearmen charged at once. One speared the intruder behind its front leg, the second behind its ribs, the third near its rear leg. Angered, the lion would bite or bat the first spear away but find itself unable to reach the other two. If the nkoma favored us it would leap back over the barrier, leaving both herd and herdsmen alive."

Into the Desert

After several seasons, the migrants left the river, turning uphill and inland into what they perceived as a desert. That decision seems odd. Why would a group of water-oriented migrants leave their only known source of water, to march into what they believed would be thorns, bush, and sand?

One reason was fear. The *mugwe* of that time had reported periodic dreams:

"The Nguo Ntune search for us daily. They move along the seaside coastal bank but search always for a place to cross. To save ourselves we must leave the river and pass through a place of hot sand and sharp thorns to reach a better land."

Another reason, however, was ecological. What the Ngaa perceived as desert was indeed a sand-and-thorn waste, but occasionally dotted with broad, shallow papyrus swamps. Each invited temporary settlement. More important, the swamps were interspersed with seasonal rivers, all originating in the Tana.

Both swamps and rivers went dry as the rains ended, thus forcing the migrants back into motion. However, by leaving the river, then moving uphill and inland, they could drift from water-point to water-point, plant, herd, fish, and then move further as the dry times began.

"As the group drifted north, west and uphill, the dry seasons grew more severe. On occasion, the people had to dig deeply into the sand

for water. Sometimes, the holes would be as deep as two men—and the labor was only beginning.

"Once water was found the hole would be widened. A narrow path had then to be carefully constructed to its bottom, to let the goats descend and drink. Each goat was then hand-led to water, since a goat-stampede towards the water at the bottom would collapse the path and perhaps the well, burying some of us."

The Migrants Fragment

Once the Ngaa had left the river to move into the desert, they began to divide into three groups. The majority remained close to water, farming, herding, and fishing. One group, however, took a different path, the *aturi* (ironsmiths). While on Mbwa, the ironsmiths were simply a part of society. The iron they used came from iron sand. It had a black, metallic luster, thus was easily found and gathered. It was smelted using triangular goatskin bellows.

There was no mystery in the production. Nor did the smiths form a separate clan. Rather, each clan had its own ironworkers, who drew apprentices from among their sons. Smiths participated in feasts, married without restriction, and had no special rituals to set them apart.

All this changed on the migration. The land adjacent to the Tana seemed to have no iron sands at all. Increasingly frustrated, the smiths began to search further and further way from the main group, gradually forming into the equivalent of a hunting band but in search of iron sands instead of animals. Their need was urgent. Iron was believed to have a life of its own, a life-force able to both harm predators and protect men. Without it they feared the wilderness, yet moved ever deeper into it.

The need for self-protection was obvious. In those days, predators were everywhere and spears did little to deter them. Instead, they turned to ritual, creating chanted curses meant initially to drive animals away, but also to protect the few, scarce sources of iron that they did find from other men.

To achieve this, the smiths would gather in darkness, on a fringe of the mainstream Ngaa community, but within earshot. Suddenly, many iron hammers would be slammed simultaneously into many iron anvils. Loud chants would accompany each bang of the hammers, intended to intimidate the mainstream cultivator/herders:

"Let he who sees black (iron) sand lose (the use of) his eyes."

No specific person was named. The goal was to frighten the entire community into avoiding the source of their work.

One result, perhaps unintended, was their progressive estrangement from the mainstream community. Cultivators and herders simply avoided the smiths who had threatened them. Deprived of companionship, the *aturi* (smiths) gathered in bands of their own, remaining part of mainstream society, but on its fringes.

The Aathi (Hunters) Emerge

Ngaa *aathi* (hunters) followed similar patterns. There were no hunters on Mbwa. Once on migration, however, the inevitable lack of grain, milk, and meat during dry seasons must have led men from the poorer clans to seek other types of food.

Banding together in the same way as the ironsmiths, they formed hunting bands, sharing whatever was scavenged or speared. As the wildlife and honey nearest the river were exhausted, they hunted inland, spending more and more time apart from the mainstream.

Aathi hunted bush meat and honey. Like the smiths, they feared attack by predators. Like the smiths, as their successes increased, they faced the problem of preserving their sources of supply. One wandering cultivator could find and ravage a beehive. One wandering man with a goat herd could disperse huge concentrations of game.

Aathi responded by expanding the traditional cursing system, reshaping it to fit their economic needs. If cursing was an individual affair on the island, the hunters collectivized it. A successful hunt, or discovery of a hive, would be followed by a feast, where everything was shared among only the hunters. Initially, these took place in the bush. Later, they were moved to the edge of the mainstream community, where the feasting could be heard.

As night fell, the hunters gathered.

"Our fire would blaze. A curse would be chanted and rechanted by all of us, followed by the unending repetition of one sound 'twiiiii, twiiiii, twiiiii , twiiiii.'"

The sound was meant to symbolize the *aathi*. It was intended to carry through the darkness into every mainstream hut.

The curse was general, never using single names. The intended punishments were both socially appropriate and physically visible, so that everyone would know who had been cursed:

"He who harms hives, let his fingers die one by one.
He who eats (bush) meat, let his teeth die (fall out) one by one."

The intended victims, having been raised to believe in the effectiveness of cursing, would know both that they had eaten one of the hunter-forbidden substances and what supernatural penalties would follow. Then, through the power of the human mind, the penalties began to occur.

The casting of curses by a single group required specialists to emerge among them to deal with the consequences. The *aathi* cursing system thus required the emergence of *aathi kiamas* (elders' councils, plural: biama) to reconcile the persons most concerned. Like the smiths, the hunters also created their own group of ritual specialists who cursed, removed curses, and divined who had been harmed.

Thus, if a victim had eaten bush meat, then experienced stomach cramps, he would visit the appropriate *aathi* ritual specialist, paying an appropriate number of goats, to have the curse removed. The hunters would feast on goats (renaming them "bushbuck") while the victim avoided further contact with wild game.

Gradually, this pattern grew into an entire series of taboos, forbidding those of one occupation to share certain foods with the other two, thus eliminating what is perhaps the single most important act of African hospitality—sharing meat. Men who ate bush meat were forbidden to touch goats, milk, or millet, even as beer. Those who did were forbidden to eat honey, honey wine, or bush meat.

One result was the elimination of both community-wide meat feasts and beer drinking, which had formed the core of male social interaction. Instead, the cultivators, hunters, and ironsmiths each feasted and drank on their own. In consequence, like the ironsmiths, the hunters remained part of migrant society, but—increasingly cloaked in mystery— they stayed on its fringes.

Many seasons passed, marked only by the periodic creation of new age-sets. By moving uphill, North, and West, the migrants must eventually have glimpsed the snow-covered peak of a shining mountain. Drawn to it, they must have moved further and further from the River Tana, approaching the gleaming mountain from the south. One day, it would be known as *Kilima kia Mara*, the shining mountain. However, that day was far in the future.

Chapter 5
Climbing Mount Kenya

Every segment of the now-fragmented Ngaa reached the base of Mt. Kenya, the Nyambeni Hills and the Tigania plain during the 1730s–1740s (*Mukuruma* age-set). What they saw must have both awed and frightened them, for the landscape lay completely outside their collective experience. Then, as now, Mt. Kenya rears up out of the arid, flat plain like a lion, crouching silently in dust. Its peaks—snow-and-ice-capped at that time—stand 17,057 feet high, providing a shining crown that must have drawn the migrants from 60 miles away.

In that era, the mountain slope was composed of ecologically distinct zones, each of which posed problems. Below the the peaks lay an open moor, consisting mainly of shallow bogs, chilling mists, and icy winds. Human survival was impossible. Below the moor lay a zone of bamboo, with groves up to 24 feet high. Older plants had partially fallen to form tangled barriers, through which younger plants struggled to grow. Except for paths opened by rhino, elephant, and buffalo, this zone was also barred to man.

Below the bamboo, however, was a zone of rainforest—which the migrants called Black Forest. Many trees had six-foot trunks, grew up to 150 feet high, and displayed a thick canopy of interlocking branches. The canopy, in turn, provided so much shade as to inhibit the development of undergrowth. As a result, wild game—and later *aathi* hunters—could slip easily through the forest in search of meat and honey.

Below the forest lay two zones of grass thinly interspersed with trees, both indicative of fertile soil. This drew both the farmers and herders, particularly since the woodland and semi-desert zones beneath these grasslands would prove less fertile.

The grass zones, however, were sharply limited by steep mountain gorges on both sides. Eons of water runoff from the higher elevations had cut deep clefts through the bedrock, many over 100 feet deep. Their slopes were difficult to descend and climb, while the rivers that raged along their bottoms were dangerous in dry seasons and impassable during rains. The ecological result was the division of the mountain slope into sharp, steep ridges that grew narrower as they rose.

The Second Fragmentation

As the migrants approached the mountain, Ngaa society began to fragment once more, first splitting into two major segments, then into smaller ones. At least one section moved toward what would later be known as the Nyambeni Mountain Range, which stretches northeast from the base of Mt. Kenya. Other groups wandered onto the Tigania plain, which lies between the Nyambenis and Mt. Kenya itself. The remainder, however, splintered into several fragments, all of whom were drawn towards the various forested ridges that may have cloaked Mt. Kenya's slopes almost down to the plains.

At least three Ngaa segments moved into the lowest sections of today's Igoji, Abogeta (S. Imenti) and Abothoguchi

(N. Imenti). Still other groups drifted South, then onto the ridges that make up today's Mwimbe and Muthambi.

Logically, the herder/cultivators settled at the base of each ridge, while the *aathi* entered the lowest fringes of the Black Forest. From that time on, each group selected a ridge of its own. Although every section of the Ngaa continued to migrate West, the only way they could really go was up. However, they did so separately, edging slowly up the ridges like a line of spears, each group out of contact with all the others. In short, the Ngaa dissolved and the name was lost to Meru history.

Why Did the Ngaa Dissolve?

The islanders-turned-migrants had remained together for generations. They had collectively survived a series of increasingly harsh environments, under-weaponed and without a goal. Why did the sight of a mountain destroy decades of social and physical unity?

One possibility is that the migrants were overwhelmed by the lure of a wholly new ecology. On migration, they had survived by finding water. On Mt. Kenya, although confined by mountain gorges, water was everywhere. Trees were everywhere and promised shade for both people and their herds, a factor that might have seemed important to migrants who had endured unending seasons in unremitting heat, thorn bush, and sand. The forests also may have promised concealment from future enemies. Grasses were abundant, as was wood for cooking fires. In essence, the choice may have been whether to go up or stay down on the arid plain.

However, they could not migrate up along the racing rivers. Steep cliffs and thick forest made them impassable. Thus, through necessity, they chose the crown of every ridgetop, moving upward where the trees were thinnest and land most easily cleared.

They climbed seasonally, but steadily. The ridgetop soil was thin. Its fertility declined with every sown crop. Millet came up stunted. The grasses were steadily exhausted, since goats pulled them up by the roots. In short, the migrants had frequently to migrate, but this time uphill, clearing off whatever vegetation barred their way. They had good reason to climb, since every move uphill brought them into cooler climate, untouched grass, and virgin soil.

Over time, the gorges became political, as well as geographic, boundaries. By settling along the narrow spines between the gorges, they set them as the limits of their land claims, moving upward (rather than outward) each time new areas were cleared. In the process, each migrant group (usually several clans) became social units themselves, losing contact with all other segments of their society. No longer did they use the word *Ngaa*. Instead, they became ridgetop communities, each with its own name, which would one day turn upon each other and make war.

Ax, Red Clay, and Firestick: Aathi "Magic" Evolves

Aathi entered what they saw as "black" forests with trepidation. They quickly learned to discard both shields and spears as too unwieldly to carry through unending, heavy vegetation. Rather, they relied on small bows, iron-tipped arrows, and iron-bladed knives. None of these, of course, protected them against a buffalo, lying silent and still within a dark thicket, or an equally silent leopard watching from a tree. Instead, they turned to ritual, gradually creating an entire series of objects which they (ritually) empowered with supernatural abilities to protect them from harm.

Bite, Blow, and Skull

The first of these was known as either "bite," or "blow." It could be prepared only by *aathi* curse-removers who had been approached by one or more hunters, bearing the traditional gifts of honey or bush meat. To prepare these substances, the *aathi* curse-remover would comb the nearby forest to gather herbs, roots, animal parts, and the sap of a specific poisonous tree. The materials would be mixed with water, then boiled until only a dark, waxy sap was left. This was either bitten (bite) or ground into powder (blow), then stored in small bamboo tubes or antelope horns.

Instructions for use were precise.

"If we saw danger, the first (leading) hunter would either "bite" or "blow" the powder in all directions. He would then chant a curse: 'Njura mno muthwa aki. Tukana gintu giku.' (Only ants on the paths. We shall see no bad things)."

The ritual had the psychological effect of creating a moving zone of safety within which the hunter could carry on his work.

This concept was subsequently adopted to create static safe zones around more permanent hunting camps. The ritual (magic) used to guard these camps was known as *nkima* (skull).

To make *nkima*, strips of buffalo, bush buck, or antelope hide were coated with the same waxy substance used to make *bite* and *blow*. The strips were then interwoven into a rounded mass the size and shape of a human skull. The "skull" then hung prominently in the center of a hunting camp, thereby psychologically creating a second zone of safety for those sleeping within.

Over time, however, the hunters faced another problem. Within a given ridgetop, all areas initially used for bush meat and honey hunting were eventually coveted by the herder/cultivators. Groups of mainstream women combed the lower regions of the forest for firewood. Groups of men cut trees to make charcoal. Groups of boys prowled forest groves, using small bows to shoot monkeys. Ritualists sought herbs, roots, leaves, and animal parts to create their medicine. If some of the intruders found beehives, how could they know if *aathi* had reached them first? Worse, all these intrusions caused wildlife to flee uphill. In consequence, the hunting bands found themselves gradually forced uphill as well.

Initially the *aathi* reacted to these encroachments by chanting the same curses they had used in the migration. However, the sheer breadth of the forest often robbed them of effectiveness. Bands of cultivators passing through the forest would never really know if they had dispersed wild game or passed a hive, thus suffered no anxiety on hearing *aathi* curses.

Bone and Claw

Eventually, the earlier system of chanting near the mainstream settlements was supplemented by ritualizing the traditional *ndindi* (firesticks), used by cultivators to mark their land and hunters to place along their hunting trails. Each stick symbolized private property, forbidding trespass.

Hunting bands selected several long sticks from a specific tree they held sacred. Each was then hollowed out at one end and sharpened at the other. The hollow space was filled with the ritualized black powder renamed either *blow* or *bite*. The feather of a marabou stork, one of the largest flying carrion eaters, was attached to the hollowed end, to suggest that the bird would devour those who angered it. Finally, the *ndindi* stick was smeared with bright red clay to enhance visibility within an eternally green forest.

Each stick was then cursed, as members of the hunting band circled it, chanting their traditional curses in unison. Thereafter, the *ndindi* were no longer simple firesticks. They became *bones*, empowered to impose a curse on every non-*aathi* who saw one. By seeing a red "bone," each cultivator would know he had penetrated an *aathi* hunting or honey zone and the curse would take effect.

This new cursing system had advantages. One was as a warning system, since even the thought of bypassing an *aathi* "bone" might keep mainstream cultivators away. The second was its automatic nature. Since the curse was automatic, hunters had no further need to either guard their zones nor terrorize the mainstream community by shouted chants along their fringes.

Instead, under the *ndindi* system, victims worked the curse upon themselves, the anxiety and guilt triggered by seeing a stick proving sufficient to induce whatever calamities they had been taught to believe must follow. The onset of these, in turn, left the victims no choice but to disclose their transgressions to the hunters themselves, since only *aathi* ritualists could remove an *aathi* curse.

When faced with defiance, *aathi* intensified the *ndindi* system. On occasion, entire mainstream communities would defy the warnings and move uphill, driven by the exhaustion of their grasses and soil. Alternately, an entire community would be forced into the forest to escape locusts, drought, or enemy attacks.

To inhibit these mass intrusions, the *ndindi* stick evolved into the *nguchwa* (claw). Claw-sticks were cut from the same sacred tree as the *ndindi*. They were hollowed on one end but split two ways at the other. The split end was then heated to make the tips curve into a claw. The hole in the center was then blocked with the tail of a mongoose, tied with a creeping tree vine.

The curse was activated in the same manner as the *ndindi*. *Nguchwa*, however, were placed in the ground, claw up, before the hut of whoever was believed to have offended *aathi*. The hunters then circled the offenders hut, chanting

"Those who eat (the food of) aathi, let them sicken."

Since the entire mainstream community would then waken, learn of the *nguchwa* and then shun the offender, instant restitution was inevitable, and the chanting *aathi* would receive hastily gathered "gifts" of millet, beer, and livestock.

Gazelle

On rare occasions, conflict would break out between entire cultivator clans and groups of hunters. This might happen when mainstream groups were forced upward into *aathi* hunting zones when migrating or in flight. In this instance, a newly killed gazelle was hollowed out in the same manner as *ndindi*:

"The gazelle body was filled with the ashes of a hyena cub, colobus monkey and keiea (a killing parasitical vine)—as well as the black powder used for 'blow' and 'bite.'"

Once ritually empowered, the hollow body of the animal was now considered a "living firestick," its flesh containing more supernatural power than wood.

The hunting band would then descend upon intruders at night, encircling the entire community, loudly chanting their curses. On waking, the victims had little choice. Either everyone would sicken, or the chanting hunters would be placated with gifts of meat—initially goats and eventually cows—which both sides renamed "bushbuck" and "buffalo"—thereby circumventing the taboo against sharing food.

At this point in Meru history, the cursing systems used by both ironsmiths and hunters differed sharply from that used by the mainstream. Herder/cultivators used curses both to harm enemies and then to reconcile. Ironsmith and hunting curses evolved solely along defensive lines. Bite, blow, skull, claw, and gazelle each reflected the efforts of numerical minorities to defend their sources of supply against a much larger mainstream majority.

However, the encroachers remained kin, sharing common ancestry, language, history and culture. Clearly, *aathi* cursing specialists made no attempt to kill or even permanently harm their mainstream kinsmen. Their goal was just to force each victim to come to them—with appropriate gifts—to have a curse removed. Therefore, the ultimate purpose of even this modified form of cursing system was to maintain harmony among cultivator/herders, ironsmiths and aathi. Once again, the sole purpose of the Meru *mugiro* (cursing system) was to maintain peace.

Chapter 6

Waging War

None of the migrating groups occupied the Mt. Kenya region without waging war. The rate and direction of their migration inevitably brought them all into contact and then conflict with earlier occupants. Evidence suggests that the pre-Meru met members of three non-Bantu cultures in small numbers, along the mountain's lower slope and northeast in the adjacent Tigania plain. Galla-speaking peoples (Oromo) drove small cattle herds along the mountain's arid base. Ogiek speakers (Kalenjin) inhabited the star-grass zone and lower forest fringes. Maa speakers (Maasai), with larger herds of cattle, commanded the Tigania plains.

There were decades of war. Each dry season led to universal cattle raiding, which intensified after the pre-Meru migrants began to acquire herds of their own. One extended battle took place when the migrants first entered the Tigania plains. Their scouts reported an entire sea of grass filled with few people and many cows.

The defenders are remembered as Mwoko. Pre-Meru raiders took the Mwoko by surprise, scattering the defenders, seizing "four great herds" and stampeding them back to their main camp. Scores of Mwoko warriors gave chase, all focused on the rescue of a single herd. The cattle, their herders, and the pursuing Muoko raced through the long grass, with warriors on both sides shedding sandals and blankets to go faster. Armed and naked, they continued the race. However, the rustlers were disadvantaged; they had to both run and herd the racing cattle in the required direction.

The Mwoko pursuers closed in. The rustlers, abandoning the herd, all turned to fight, shields and spears in hand. Many spear thrusts led to many wounds but no casualties, as the heavy, awkward spears were often easily pushed aside by shield thrusts. At this point, the pre-Meru were joined by comrades who had heard the shouting. The two sides separated as the rustlers seized the herd.

The Mwoko, initially outnumbered, reacting by barring the intruders from both water and salt, systematically burying salt licks and springs to prevent their discovery and use. They also had large-tipped stabbing spears with which to protect their remaining herds. The pre-Meru responded with bow and arrow, ambushing Mwoko herders in the long grass and stampeding the cattle.

This pattern was repeated across the entire line of advance. Groups would make contact, then launch dry-season raids—moving cattle back and forth between them, with minimal casualties on both sides. In the wet seasons, women moved back and forth between hostile communities, bearing not only trade goods but the possibility of alliance through marriage.

On balance, the pre-Meru acquired several useful goods and concepts from those with whom they fought. One, obviously, was the acquisition of large numbers of cattle. A second was adopting better weapons—larger spears, and using barbs on the iron tips of arrows. This was particularly true when the advancing migrants met and clashed with large groups of Maasai, both in Tigania and the Northern base of the mountain. The two sides fought with results comparable to the combat with Mwoko. Raids were launched in every dry season, as each side strove to seize the other's flocks and herds.

One result of this recurrent interaction was that the Maasai gave the pre-Meru their name. In Maa (the Maasai language) the word *miru* means both "cold and dark" and "silent and still." The term referred both to the forests in which most of the migrants lived and the migrants themselves, who were seen as "cold, dark, silent, and still" (USA: hostile and stupid) because they spoke no Maa. Over time, the word was accepted and became *Meru*. Beyond that, pre-Meru warriors in every region adopted aspects of Maasai warfare: hair style, mode of dress, longer spear heads, wooden clubs, and buffalo-skin shields. More important, they adopted Maasai military ideals: pursuit of cattle as a proof of manhood and the seasonal waging of a highly stylized method of war.

Learning How: Rules of War

Imitating the Maasai, the Meru fought under a system of military conventions (ancestral traditions), intended both to provoke and limit war. War was fought to acquire livestock; nothing else. Cattle, sheep and goats could be taken. Ripening crops, however, could neither be seized or destroyed. Raiders passing through a foe's banana groves might snatch what they could eat, but not cut the trees. Others, driving stolen cattle across fields of millet or yams would be "sued" for crop damage, once the conflict ended, with the amount (repaid in livestock) set by elders on both sides.

Nor could raiders plunder homesteads. They might move through a group of huts, peering into each to see what could be seized, but not burn the huts themselves. Tradition also defined what could be taken. Spears, clubs and other weapons were considered trophies of war. Farming, herding and household tools were not. Nor were beads, cloth, honey, salt, meat, or other potential trade goods. War was not waged for profit, but livestock and glory.

Other military traditions served to preserve human life. Harming the aged and young was forbidden. Women could be taken captive. However, if unmarried, they were given (by the elders) to their captors as daughters, later to be ransomed for cattle. If married, they became their captors' wives, unless exchanged for cattle. If they stayed, their husbands would eventually receive bride wealth from the captive's father, thus cementing each woman's position in the new society.

Male captives followed the same traditions. Surrender was standardized.

*"If two warriors fought, the weaker could either shout
'ngua ng'ombe' (take cattle!) or raise his weapons points up,
then push them towards his opponent."*

The victor would seize them, tear off his own skin cloak and place it on his captive's shoulders, thus symbolically eliminating him from the fight. The captured warrior was then honor-bound to follow his captor home. There he remained, until—with the battle concluded—elders from both sides met to negotiate the number of cows to be exchanged, both for captives and to pay for damage. Only after agreement was reached were hostilities considered at an end.

Another tradition inhibited killing. Although capturing someone meant acquiring cattle, killing an opponent, even in battle, cost the killer livestock from his father's herds. A killing automatically placed the warrior under a curse. That, in turn, shut him off from his community and required the sacrifice of livestock to remove. In short, killing cost the killer cattle.

Another entire set of conventions operated to make raiding virtually inevitable. No herds, for instance, were ever hidden in thick forest, placed behind log barricades or concealed in pits. Rather, family herds were gathered together at dusk and driven onto grassland, to be guarded by the least experienced warriors. All others slept in a *gaaru* (warrior barrack), near enough to seize weapons if attacked, but far enough for herds to be a tempting target. To defend effectively would dishonor the defenders, since only conflict could bring both sides the chance of honor.

A warrior's reward was the acquisition of a praise name. Whatever cattle he acquired went into his father's herd, rewarded only by a promise to eventually use the animals to find his son a bride. At night, however, feasting began, followed by a praise dance. Each warrior who had taken trophies or captured livestock danced in turn onto the field, singing of what he had done. The mother of each man stepped forward to strip off his skin cloak, and he stood, armed and naked, while the women of his ridgetop chanted the praise name by which he would thereafter be known.

The Ridgetops Turn on Each Other

A time came when these traditions of limited war became so attractive that the ridgetop communities turned on one another, and cattle raiding became a blood sport. They did this by dividing into "opponents" and "allies." Three chains of alliance emerged among the Meru, each reflecting both military and ancestral ties remembered from the past. Tigania allied with Mwimbe, reflecting an earlier period when both groups had formed a unit known as Murutu

"Tigania, Mwimbe and Murutu were once one."

Igembe, Imenti, Igoji and Muthambi formed a second alliance, reflecting a time when they had been united as Mukungu.

"Igoji, Igembe, Imenti and Muthambi were once one."

A third chain consisted of two Meru neighbors (Chuka to the south and Tharaka to the east) as well as a tiny region between Igoji and Imenti known as Miutini.

In theory, every ridgetop could have acquired total protection by forming alliances with every Meru on the mountain. To do so, however, would have left no one against whom to wage war and thus no honorable way to acquire cattle. The system required that certain ridgetops remain potentially hostile, therefore providing new sources of livestock each raiding season.

Warfare was essentially the same when waged outside Meru. Raiding tactics, whether directed against other ridgetops or cattle peoples on the plains, stressed speed, stealth, silence, planning, herding, and successful evasion, rather than the European pattern of bloodshed, plunder, destruction, and complete defeat. To "win" meant the silent, bloodless, and undiscovered rustling of an opponent's herds, driving them home and, leaving the target community intact, angry, and plotting counterraids.

Cattle Raiding: Chuka vs. Mwimbe

One battle illustrates the pleasure all sides took in war. A force from Chuka successfully invaded Mwimbe, seizing entire herds. To return, however, both raiders and cattle needed to cross the river that ran between their territories. The Mwimbe pursuers, knowing the terrain, knew the herds could only cross the river at a single, shallow ford. Using shortcuts unknown to the Chuka, the pursuers reached the river first, forming a line of spears to block the raiders.

The Chuka, seeing the trap, decided to run the cattle into the river and right over the defenders. The Mwimbe, anticipating the tactic, expanded their defensive line:

"Each man moved apart from his brothers to allow cows to run between us."

The cows, desperate to avoid contact with men, did so. The Mwimbe then closed their lines, spears facing outward once again.

The Chuka charged. Both lines disintegrated into pushing, shouting, stabbing pairs, as warriors on both sides tried to either hook their opponent's shield, moving it aside to allow a spear thrust, or break a wooden shield rim with blows from a war club. In this instance, the Chuka chose not to stand and fight, but broke through the Mwimbe defensive line, racing after and eventually retrieving the fleeting cattle. Here, as so often happened, both sides suffered many spear wounds and no casualties.

In summary, Meru warfare was a hugely satisfying system. It was a universally beloved sport; one in which every warrior could expect to win chanted public praise from women, respect from elders, admiration from boys who yearned to be warriors and—eventually—sufficient cattle to form the bride wealth that would allow every warrior marriage and a family.

Chapter 7
Achunku: White Men

The first Whites to reach Meru either came with or led large trading caravans. After the 1860s, Swahili, Somali, and Coastal Arab caravans came to certain parts of Meru every dry season. They stopped to offer cloth, trinkets, and coastal beads for tusks, honey, and sufficient goats, cattle, and grain to feed their porters.

These exchanges were noisy, pleasurable, and routine. Both sides traded using similar rules. One side would set articles (or animals) in front of the other. That side would match it with objects (or animals) of its own. If both sides agreed, the trade was made. If either side objected, a period of shouting, arm waving, boastful threats, and loud laughter would lead to the provision of additional (or new) objects. Since both sides truly wanted to trade, bargaining and arguing gave pleasure to everyone.

White Traders; White (Trading) Rules

Those Europeans who first joined the caravans and then led them initially saw themselves as part of this commercial pattern, wanting only to maintain it. Their caravans stopped in Meru to hunt and trade trinkets for tusks, herds, flocks, and millet before traveling beyond the Mountain. Unfortunately, European ideas of trading differed sharply from those of Meru. One rule was that transactions take place instantly. African traditions of pleasant days spent bargaining were beyond the Europeans' mental reach. Once they had offered what they felt to be adequate quantities of trade goods they expected the offer to be instantly accepted and the Meru trade goods (herds, flocks, etc.) to instantly appear. Any delay in negotiations—or worse, a refusal to trade—was considered an act of war.

One illustration of this pattern is found in the behavior of Karl Peters, a German who reached neighboring Tharaka in 1889. Angered by their rejection of his initial trading offer, he plundered 600 head of cattle then literally shot his way out of the district, killing as many warriors as possible.

A more detailed example can be seen in the actions of Wm. Astor Chanler, an American who reached Igembe in 1892. To ensure trading success, he seized two "old men" as hostages. In so doing, he violated Igembe military conventions, which restricted hostilities to warriors and captivity to women. When a unit of 50 outraged warriors appeared, Chanler scattered them with gunfire, seizing four as hostages. He then demanded trade!

Predictably, the Igembe called for reinforcements from every neighboring clan. The next morning, Chanler found his caravan ringed by over 400 spearmen, spoiling to fight. In this moment of crisis, Igembe elders intervened, effectively redirecting the caravan to neighboring Tigania.

Forewarned, hundreds of Tigania warriors surrounded it, reinforced by junior elders carrying bows and poison-tipped arrows. Chanler decided to fight. After taking another ruling elder hostage, he sent foraging parties to scour the villages for goats, sheep, and cattle. Two hundred warriors blocked the foragers' return. Rifle fire broke the blockade, leaving 30 dead.

Thereafter the caravan marched back to Igembe, surrounded by a moving screen of enraged Tiganian pursuers, raining poison arrows on the column from the thorn bush.

The Igembe elders, thoroughly alarmed to see Chanler return, offered *gichiaro*, the creation of both blood brotherhood and military alliance between both sides. As symbolic brothers, the caravan could not be attacked. Having collected sufficient livestock and grain, Chanler moved on.

This pattern of livestock plunder, warrior counter attack, rifle fire, elders' intervention and finally *gichiaro* was repeated for the next decade by every European caravan to enter Meru. In each case, the elders' decision for peace on the intruders' terms enraged the warriors, who "rose to their feet and danced in fury." Yet, in the end they always submitted. As required by tradition.

Natural Calamities Strike

There were reasons for this perpetual submission, some going deeper than a simple fear of rifles. Beginning in the late 1880s an unprecedented series of natural calamities struck every ridgetop in Meru, decimating both livestock and people in such numbers as to significantly weaken their ability to wage war.

In 1887–88, Meru cattle herds were decimated by the rinderpest epidemic that swept through African cattle communities from Sudan to South Africa. In 1891, the upland millet crops were stunted by drought, while the drier lowland crops were devastated. Both lowland millet and grasses were then destroyed by overwhelming swarms of locusts. In 1892, the near-starving ridgetops were decimated by smallpox, striking with sufficient ferocity to disperse entire clans.

The social consequence, inevitably, was the emergence of a rural proletariat, bereft of livestock, temporarily landless, and even deprived of kin. The young men in this steadily expanding group inevitably shifted their focus away from warriorhood and towards survival.

The Mugiro (Curse) Evolves

Cultivators living closest to the forest found themselves increasingly influenced by *aathi* cursing rituals. The natural catastrophes that decimated Meru herds and crops were much more intense in the lowlands, where semi-starvation was widespread. Gradually, the upland cultivators began to experience the appearance of hungry hordes from the lower slopes, either creeping among their remaining crops at night, or sweeping through them at dusk.

Uplander *kiamas* turned to the *aathi*, bartering goats (relabeled "bushbuck") for ritual knowledge. Once gained, they became known as the "*kiamas* of crop protection." In Muthambi, for example, an *aaathi kiama* carved seven *ndindi* sticks from the hunter's sacred tree. These were bundled together, daubed with red ochre, then tied with a gazelle-skin sandal.

The bundle was passed to an uplander in exchange for a goat. With it, the hunter passed on the rituals needed to make the power in the sticks impose a curse on any other cultivators passing near his crop. A large field required many bundles, exchanged for many goats.

Knowledge of the bundles spread in traditional Meru fashion. Every elder who received one sought out fellow elders, "selling" his knowledge to those elders willing to join him in forming a crop-protectors' *kiama*, now recalled as Wathua.

Eventually, these *kiamas* adopted a long, wire-thin vine, taken from the same tree held sacred by *aathi*, and used by hunters when creating the curse of *kallai* (gazelle). The cultivators simply looped the vine around several of their *ndindi* bundles to completely rim their fields. To see the vine was to suffer the curse.

Kiamas of the Stomach

Crop protection only intensified the problems of lowland cultivators, many of whom had lost every source of food. Hungry and angry, many banded together into a number of small bands (Wathi, Kagita, Muundu, etc.), collectively known as "*kiamas* of the stomach." Faced with ruin, they acquired knowledge of the *aathi* rituals from Wathua kinsmen, then transformed them to meet their needs.

The first step was to create a safety zone where members of a stomach *kiama* could gather and feast. Borrowing once more from *aathi* practice, they planted an *ndindi* stick, (always taken from the sacred athi tree) in the center of a clearing. They then circled the clearing, chanting repeated curses and sprinkling liquid goat dung around its edges, the smell serving to keep intruders out, as the crop protectors had used sticks and vines.

They then constructed a large, circular, banana-leaf hut, sufficient to hold 15 men. From its roof, they hung a sacred gourd, the symbolic substitute for the *aathi* "skull." The static "safety zone" was then both ritually and physically complete.

"Now it is Our Turn to Eat"

The next step was to acquire sufficient food on which to feast. Some stomach *kiamas* placed *ndindi* sticks and liquid goat dung across the public paths. Those who crossed over were forced to pay the *kiama* goats to remove the curse. Other stomach groups were more direct. The Wathua (stomach society) of Igembe, for example, selected one wealthy victim, then surrounded his homestead at night. Circling his huts, they ritually isolated the homeowner by sprinkling liquid goat dung in the same manner used to protect their meeting place. Thereafter, they gathered before the victim's door to demand a feast. Once sufficient honey beer, meat, and millet were provided they removed the curse:

"Tubu turika! Tubu Turika! Uma, mugiro wa gukiranga wathi."
(Clay pot, burst! Clay pot, burst! Curse, get out. Get out, curse
of aathi).

They feasted, then chose another victim.

Mwaa: Kiamas of Clowns

While many hungry men formed stomach *kiamas*, using ritual to extort whatever food could be found, many others blended the powers of both magic and music to provide members with food and a type of social status. These, spreading across every Meru ridgetop, became known as *mwaa*, or *kiamas* of clowns. In KiMeru (the Meru language) *waa* means both stupid and foolish (display of stupidity). A man of *waa* (*Mu-waa* or *Mwaa*) was one who publicly displays foolishness. However, the term carries overtones of clownishness, in which stupidity is displayed to make people laugh.

Each dry season, small groups of former cultivators and warriors would band together as clowns, dancing, shouting, and singing through surrounding homesteads, seeking their sustenance in the way of European minstrels. Initially, they received handfuls of nuts, castor seeds, and fruit, flung into their goatskin pouches for each burst of song.

However, the many *kiamas* of *mwaa* eventually evolved into both polished entertainers and predatory deviants. Their dancing costumes became feminine, consisting of bead-strings worn in female fashion and skirts made of shredded goatskins. Each member also wore the wide shoulder-blade of a cow across his chest. A wooden cowbell, tied around his throat, lay on the cow bone. When dancing, the bone and bell provided a basic rhythm. It was supplemented by the whistle of a *karambeta*, half-flute, half-horn, made from a hollowed stick attached to a small gourd.

Performances began at dusk, as hungry men returned from their fields for supper. The *mwaa* were also hungry. A group would dance its way into a wealthy homestead, surrounding the main hut while singing, cavorting, and chanting curses in expectation of a reward. Over time, the earlier handfuls of nuts and seeds expanded into a feast, for which cultivators were required to donate enough millet beer, beans, and goats to feed the entire troop.

Failure to donate what the *mwaa* believed to be enough led to the placing of an unusual curse on the homestead. Surrounding the main hut, the troop would purposely defecate, ringing the property with liquefied human feces that could be both smelled and seen. To remove the curse, the cultivators provided whatever additional food and beer the *mwaa* required.

Mwaa also drew spectators. Their rough, sexual songs and wild dancing brought people from everywhere within hearing range to enjoy the show. The songs mocked the host, describing (in one example) his sexual exploits when hunting buffalo, with the sound of "shots" consisting of the air expelled from their assembled anuses.

The dancing was female. The humor came from the dancer's skill in imitating female body movements, especially sexual intercourse. When combined with song and story,

"It was too great a burden not to laugh."

Some men joined *mwaa* for sexual reasons, lured by the chance to wear women's clothes and use female body movements with a group and in ways that brought at least minimal social approval. Others simply wearied of the drought-seared, locust-laden land, and being hungry. Still others, saddened that the massive loss of cattle eliminated the point of waging war, took to song, dance, and feasting as an alternative to doing nothing.

Clearly, Meru supernatural practices continued to evolve. The *mugiro* began as a tool used to regulate conflicts between individuals, using cursing rituals to cause harm, remove the curse, detect the curser, and solicit *kiama* judgments to resolve each conflict.

Mugiro rituals then evolved into a means of protecting sources of honey and meat for hunters. Thereafter, the curse became a form of crop-protection. Widespread famine caused it to evolve into a tool for extorting food. Finally, it became a means of protecting sexual deviation in a society where none had ever been allowed.

The natural catastrophes of this period sharply weakened Meru military power. Crop losses demoralized the cultivators. Cattle losses demoralized the warriors, eliminating the chance to raid. Men in both groups turned to the dancing deviants. These were, however, bad years for Meru to militarily decline. Rumors repeatedly swept across each ridgetop of an advancing military power bent on conquest.

Chapter 8

The Moment of Conquest

Caravans penetrated most Meru regions throughout the 1890s. Each arrival precipitated increasingly severe conflict between warriors and elders. Warriors viewed each intrusion as a chance to gain livestock and glory. Elders, however, saw each caravan as composed of seekers of plunder and death, thus refused all warrior demands to attack.

The elders' fears were intensified by the stories passed on to Meru by caravan porters—tales of warfare against both Maasai and Gikuyu—large, powerful tribes to Meru's South and East. Each story spoke of sticks that threw fire at a distance, the capture of elders, the harming of children, destruction of homes, banana groves, millet fields, and sometimes whole communities. These acts were both so savage and far removed from Meru military traditions that they were hard to believe. Wilder stories followed; Gikuyu and Maasai warriors were said to have laid aside their spears for women's digging sticks, to dig paths that looked like snakes across the ridges and north towards Meru.

The Battle of Embu

Meru fears peaked after 1906, as they learned of the conquest of neighboring Embu. Embu-speaking peoples lived south of Chuka, which lay south of the Meru-speaking regions. Defiant in the shelter of their mountain forest, Embu had long refused to deal with Europeans, attacking their caravans and refusing them food. They had acquired a number of workable guns, which gave them a confidence above their military capacities.

The British wanted Embu because they objected to any hostile force near their own. Gikuyu and Maasai, recently conquered and now subordinate allies, had lost their own cattle to British power. Thus, they thirsted after Embu herds. The British sent a message to an Embu war leader, one of many, demanding 1,000 cattle and an apology for past transgressions. The Embu returned the paper with a basket of millet, asking the invaders to count each grain if they wished to learn how many warriors awaited the invaders.

Embu contempt for European power was then displayed by a decision to ignore it, instead launching a massive raid on Chuka. Several hundred raiders crossed the Chuka-Embu River, expecting to launch several simultaneous cattle raids.

The Chuka were prepared. As the weakest military society on Mt. Kenya, they had constructed immense forest barriers along the river separating them from Embu. Adding to existing forest cover, they had felled scores of trees along the riverbanks, piling them in semi-horizontal rows. They then wove thorn bush into the gaps.

Over time, trees and thorn bush had grown together to form living walls that ran along the Chuka borders from the plains to the forest. In some places, however, the Chuka themselves had cut twisting paths through the walls, to permit their own warriors to emerge and raid in Embu.

Embu war leaders countered this tactic by sending picked warriors, related to distant Chuka kinsmen, as spies to learn where one of the paths had been cut. Slipping through the gap in single file, they emerged into a clear area, a short run from the nearest herds.

The Chuka were waiting. Embu raiders emerged to find a large and steadily increasing force of Chuka defenders. Although fighting steadily for much of a morning, the raiders were gradually forced back into the narrow path without a single cow.

Thirsty, weary, angry, and depressed by their defeat, the raiders were met on the Embu side of the barrier by runners from their home communities. Hysterical and exhausted, the messengers gasped out that they had been invaded and their cattle and women were being seized. Stunned by the news, the entire body of warriors set off at a dead run.

The raiders arrived, exhausted from both their prior battle and the speed of their return. They found their entire homeland in chaos with enemies everywhere. Invaders had penetrated at five points along the Gikuyu-Embu border, then spread out to seize women, flocks, and herds.

Initially perceiving this as a Gikuyu invasion, the exhausted Embu launched a traditional counter-attack, splintering their larger force into smaller groups racing off to protect their herds and homesteads. The heart of the invasion force, however, was a unit of the Kings African Rifles. Led by three Europeans, it consisted of 200 "alien Africans," drawn from distant British colonies such as Sudan. Unable to speak to the peoples they conquered, the aliens made obedient and effective soldiers. All were armed with breech-loading rifles, with higher rates of fire than any the Embu had seen.

In consequence, each subsequent attempt to reconcentrate the Embu defenders was scattered by rifle fire. Single Embu fought with notable courage, often charging directly into the rifles, shouting that they could only shoot water. However, resistance swiftly crumbled and Gikuyu and Maasai raiders spread unchecked among the Embu herds.

For nine days, Embu warriors hid and starved in the forests, while their various enemies drove off over 10,000 cattle, sheep, and goats. Every military convention was violated: hundreds of livestock were uselessly slaughtered. Banana groves and millet fields were razed. Women were seized, elders and children beaten. Warriors attempting to surrender in traditional fashion were shot or speared. It took nine days for the three Whites to control their allies and establish order.

The sheer intensity of the destruction went far beyond every Embu rule of war. It terrorized them into complete submission. It also terrorized their Meru-speaking neighbors to the North.

Meru: Bloodless Conquest

British power expanded Northward into Meru in 1907, led by Edward Butler Horne, then 26 years old, leading one 100-man company of Kings African Rifles, supported by Maasai spearmen. Gikuyu and Embu accompanied him as porters. Horne was physically short, just over five feet, and many Africans called him *Bwana Kidogo* (little master, but also used to refer to a child). To both compensate for his size and intimidate his probable opponents, he led the invasion on a large, white horse.

The invaders were preceded, however, by the arrival of fleeing Embu, kinsmen to families in Chuka, Mwimbe and Muthambe, driving the remnants of their livestock to safety with their Meru kin. The herds were followed by steady trickles of refugees, the aged, women, and children fleeing to safety, their homes burned. The refugees told stories that terrified everyone. The most frightening were their stories of the White man's *bunduki* (gun):

"If you stand behind a tree, you are killed. If you stand behind a shield, you are killed. If you stand behind a hill, you are killed."

The most senior *kiamas* of Mwimbe and Muthambi combined in a single meeting to argue for days, caught between the desire for courage and their fear of its consequences. They sent their own kinsmen into Embu to learn the truth, only to have them return to report defeat and devastation. Finally, the psychological weight of a decade of prophecies, combined with the crushing of two larger and more powerful neighbors, finally penetrated their collective thinking. They decided to ask for peace.

To them, "peace" meant handing over a reasonable portion of their flocks and herds and allowing the invaders to move on. That decision, however, was opposed by the combined warrior contingents of Mwimbe and Muthambe, who had joined together in a single field, to dance, chant war-songs, and shout out vows to crush all enemies.

Horne Appears; Muthambe Submits

Horne had been instructed to establish Colonial authority in Chuka, Muthambe, Mwimbe and Igoji. Proceeding through Chuka without incident, his force appeared in upper Muthambi, and was guided to the place where the most senior Mwimbe and Muthambi *kiamas* sat together in council.

He was greeted by Njage wa Kathiori, a notable Muthambe war leader. Learning of Horne's impending arrival, Njage had hidden all the warriors within a fringe of the surrounding forest. Horne asked him,

"If they call you war-leader, where are your warriors?"
"They are hiding, Njage answered, "lest their fierceness frighten the White man who has come as a guest."
"I have not come as a guest," Horne declared. "I have come to rule. Bring your warriors to me, now."

They appeared, spears banging in unison against shields and hurling battle cries at the invaders. Horne immediately demonstrated his gun. First, he killed a bull, standing far away. Then, he asked Njage if a spear could penetrate his buffalo-hide shield. Njage said it was impossible. Then, Horne asked for six shields to be stacked together against a tree. His bullet penetrated them all. The demonstrations brought the warriors to shocked silence.

Horne then asked who led them.

The reply was "Our elders' kiama."
"How to you deal with your neighbors," Horne continued.

"By war," the shout came from 100 throats. "We take their cattle."
Horne's reply: "I have been sent by my King to bring peace. All cattle-
raiding is to stop. All quarrels between peoples will be set before me to
judge, rather than settled with clubs and spears."

At this, the warriors sent up a concerted howl of rage, asking with 100 voices how they were to acquire the cattle they needed for brides.

"Through trade." Horne replied. "But you will not be idle. A great
path is being built across the mountain, which someday will go
around it. Every man must join the work and dig."

This raised another angry outburst as scores of warriors shouted that digging was the work of women.

"Now it is the work of men," Horne answered briefly. "Begin."

Horne then asked Njage to name the other "chiefs" in his region. Misunderstanding, the war leader named three war leaders, who led warrior bands on three other Muthambe ridgetops. Horne then proclaimed all four as "chiefs," providing Njage with a black blanket to symbolize his new authority.

No one understood the term. Njage asked what a chief did.

"He commands," Horne replied. "I will command you and you will
command your people."
"We are warriors," Njage replied.
"We are led by our elders. Show me a tribe where the kids lead the

goats and I will show you a ridgetop of madmen."
"Now, war is done," Horne declared. "I alone will lead."

Horne then commanded Njage to select the largest warriors to join his invading force, while he visited the other Muthambe regions, then moved North to Mwimbe and Igoji. At each stop, the pattern was the same: Horne would demonstrate the power of the rifle. His speech, never changing, stated that his King had sent him to end war, dig roads, and command the newly appointed "blanket chiefs."

The warrior contingents submitted without exception, each group obeying the commands of their respective elders not to fight. Only single warriors fought back. One warrior challenged Horne to single combat, bellowing like a bull, throwing-spear held at the ready. He was shot. Two warriors threw rocks at him as he rode past. Their family huts were burned; their flocks and herds seized. One man swung a long yam stem at Horne's head, hitting and unseating him. Every hut in that area was burned; every cow taken. When neighboring reinforcements arrived to help, four warriors were shot. That message spread across Meru. Resistance died.

Horne's expedition continued Northward, eventually subjugating each major ridgetop from Chuka to Igembe. He chose Imenti as his base, where he ruled for 10 years. In later times, the Meru would think back on his endless wandering, and refer to him as *Kangangi* (little walker). He is recalled only as *Kangangi* today.

Chapter 9
The Tragedy of Colonialism

The yam-stem incident had made Horne aware of his military limitations. He thus decided to construct a permanent and defensible camp. Moving his force to Imenti, he close a ridge near the Kazita river, just below the forest edge. It was high, sharply defined, and thus easily defended. It lay near permanent water and close enough to the forest to provide logs for a stockade.

Imenti elders noted that the proposed camp would lie adjacent to forest groves held sacred to the *nkoma*. Their hope was that Horne and his men would harm the grove, thereby exposing them to ancestral curses and subsequent calamity. They were initially encouraged when Horne refused to placate the ancestral spirits by sacrificing goats, then uniformly depressed when his health stayed unchanged.

Horne shrugged off their warnings, forcing Imenti warriors to log the grove, cutting trees in sufficient numbers to build two Canadian-style log cabins, one a home and the other an office. Thereafter, a "British Square" of thatch huts was constructed. Warriors were then set to digging a six-foot-deep trench around the square. Finally, river water was diverted into the trench, home, and office, and the camp was complete.

Creating Kamuchunku : Little (Colonialist) Whites

Horne then created a colonial administration. His initial seizure of authority had been backed only by the Kings

African Rifles, Maasai spearmen, and Gikuyu porters. His first step, therefore, was to supplement his non-Meru force with Meru warriors.

He began by selecting a blanket chief to rule each ridgetop, selecting muscular men of great height. Since Meru had many ridgetops, he selected many chiefs—at one point up to 91. The resulting confusion was resolved by demoting most of them to "blanket headmen," while retaining the few that he preferred.

"We (each blanket chief) received a black blanket, so that other men knew we were chiefs. Each chief was then told to select two more warriors to serve him as "blanket askari." (police). Not enough! Slowly, slowly, we (chiefs) added more askari, until soon we each had small armies."

Each *askari* also received a black blanket. Each was allowed to retain his spear and shield, a privilege which soon became important as Horne subsequently disarmed everyone else. In addition, the *askari* of each ridgetop were also permitted to construct a warrior *gaaru* (war-barrack) next to the official headquarters, within which they could behave like the warriors of tradition, eating beef, singing, and shouting out battle vows.

Blanket chiefs and *askari* alike soon discovered they had no duties other than to provide Horne with a fixed number of warrior-laborers each day, to dig whatever he wanted dug. In consequence, the blanket-wearers were initially met with universal contempt by warrior age-mates, who derided them in songs and chants as *kachunku*, small Whites.

The derision disappeared, however, when warriors on every ridgetop discovered that *kachunku* had been given the power to force them to dig what was to become known as "Horne's Road." This was a roadbed ten feet wide. It was to run across all Meru, from Embu to Igembe, and eventually around the entire mountain to Gikuyu. Every warrior on every ridgetop was to dig it. In some regions, the work was little more than clearing paths. In others, however, the road led down and then up the steep gorges, crossed racing rivers, and passed through thick forests. No European tools were available. Axes and shovels were still in the future. That left *pangas* (bush knives), made of local iron, to cut the trees, and digging sticks to uproot rocks.

Nor were the warriors cooperative. Their spokesmen repeatedly explained to Horne that digging was women's work, while men stood guard. Horne repeatedly refused. He came from a world in which men dug, women languished and (male) idleness was sin. Accordingly, he told the spokesmen that:

"women's work was making homes and children; men's duty—to battle idleness by seeking useful labor."

Horne decreed that every chief provide fixed numbers of workers at each sunrise. Chiefs passed the actual recruiting to their *askari*, appointing as many as required to do the job. In exchange, neither chiefs nor *askari* were required to work themselves.

The recruiting system, however, soon was riddled with corruption. Individual warriors soon learned that providing their *askari* with a goat or gourd of millet beer might lead to a day without work. However, prices rose swiftly, as first one and then all *askari* began to demand access to women in a warrior's household. Once at work, however, both slackness and resistance was punished by the whip, with warriors being whipped before their women in defiance of tradition.

The road crept steadily onward, but warriorhood itself began to die. The transformation of war leaders into small-scale tyrants, drunkards, and sexual exploiters destroyed all thought of both warrior discipline and united resistance. The transformation of the warrior role from raiders—a task intended to enhance their manliness—to diggers—a role reserved entirely for women—crushed their image of themselves. Horne and those Whites in authority above him may have believed they were bringing "civilization" into Africa. In fact, they brought only universal misery.

Destroying Warriorhood

Horne then turned his efforts towards what he saw as the complete elimination of war, and thus the thoroughly desirable transformation of all warriors into workers—thereby providing the British with a no-cost workforce. His first step was to both forbid and then severely punish the act of cattle raiding.

Horne did this by requiring his blanket chiefs and *askari* to report the appearance of "alien" cattle in their locations. These reports were supplemented by the acts of informers, glad to offer information in exchange for a small reward of livestock. In addition, the "losers" in a cattle-raid soon learned that reporting the loss might lead Horne to order the rustled cattle returned. Warriors accused of stealing cattle were then whipped and imprisoned. More important, their warrior hairstyle was shaved, a staggering blow to every cattle-raider whose self-image was based on his appearance.

After 1908, these earlier measures were supplemented by restrictions on physical movement. As the boundaries of each location were mapped, it was designated as a native reserve. A pass system was then imposed on the inhabitants, similar to that used in South Africa. No "native" could leave the reserve for any reason, except with permission of his chief and carrying a *chiti* (chit, pass) describing his reason for departure. No one was allowed to travel uphill into the forest, which was reserved for the Crown. Travel in groups was forbidden.

Thus, raiding became impossible. Seasonal movement of cattle to the star-grass areas was forbidden. Raids by single warriors were exposed and met by mass whippings of entire warrior units. Worse, more and more warriors found themselves spending every day of the dry (raiding) season digging the road instead of raiding. In consequence, raids died away.

The tradition of proclaiming *authi* (battle vows) died as well, along with the magnificent bull-feasts, songs, chants, and dancing that accompanied it. Before the conquest, the public battle-vow had been the culmination of an entire series of rites, intended to bring warriors to the psychological peak required to risk their lives in war.

Before each raid the warriors would isolate themselves within their *gaaru* and devour the meat of bull after bull—supplied silently by their fathers—to build up strength for the impending ordeal. As they ate they sang as one, to join themselves together as a single fighting unit. Finally, with their courage and unity at peak, they would burst free of isolation, racing fully armed to the dancing ground. There, they "danced *authi*," a bounding stiff-legged dance in which each warrior in turn would cast aside the skins that cloaked his body. Armed and naked, he would dance before the women and elders, shouting out his battle vow:

"If I return without cows, may this oath kill me!"

Horne initially responded by permitting the dancing but requiring each warrior to blood their spears on goats instead of men. He also forbade the nakedness, demanding they cover their loins while dancing. Finally, he forbade the oaths themselves. It was enough. Shorn of both sexual symbolism and military purpose, the bull feasts, songs, *authi* dancing and battle vows all died away.

The tradition of bearing weapons met the same fate. Despite the conquest, no warrior ever went without his shield and spear, both symbolizing his manhood. Yet, the very presence of weapons compelled their use, if not against enemies then among themselves. As a result, although war was forbidden, military training continued, as warrior battled warrior in vain attempts to retain military pride.

Military, Social, and Sexual Discipline Die

Inevitably, military discipline ebbed, as warrior feelings of rage and frustration exploded against their age-mates. What was originally combat training evolved into large-scale brawls, in which neighboring war bands threw themselves against each other in a frenzy of violence that neither tradition nor protesting elders could stop.

Eventually, Horne responded by banning weapons altogether, except those in the service of his King. He began this process by inviting several bands to come together to dance *authi*, with him supplying the bulls. When the assembled warriors had feasted, and their movements were slowed, Horne accused them of violating their own military traditions by brawling and injuring one another. He then ordered them to abandon their arms, stating that he alone would keep the peace. The warriors' united roar of rage was cut short by Horne's shouted command. Startled, they found themselves under the guns of the King's African Rifles.

That single incident had its intended effect on all other military contingents. Horne's subsequent commands to disarm were met with sullen compliance. Some evaded the rules, giving up old weapons while keeping new. Others buried them. However, it was hopeless. No longer could a shield and spear be carried openly as a display of warrior pride. Nor, without weapons, could new warriors be trained. The loss of weapons, open raiding, *authi* dancing, bull feasts and battle vows meant the death of every military value that had given warrior life its joy.

Drunkeness, Sex, Abortions, and Fatherless Children

The impact on military social conventions was devastating. Deprived of every reason for personal restraint, they threw aside every facet of their traditional codes of conduct. The first to crumble was the rule against drinking. Drinking, whether millet beer or honey wine, was reserved to elders. Elders got drunk knowing that their warrior sons were sober, thus alert against surprise attack. Conversely, these sons took pride in their years of abstinence, knowing that drunkeness might mean the loss of every herd.

After 1908, warriors across Meru began to drink—and drink. Neither their elders' protests nor Horne's whippings had any affect. Worse, drunkenness spread from warriors to the ranks of unmarried girls. Horne, deeply concerned, decreed that any woman and warrior found drunk together would be whipped together—a profound humiliation for the warrior, to suffer a woman's punishment lying next to a woman.

One day later, a drunken couple was brought in. Horne was painfully embarrassed but stayed true to his word. Ordering the pair to lie together on the ground, he whipped the man, but timidly tapped the girl. For a week, drinking by unmarried girls stopped dead. However, the problem was too deeply rooted to be cured. All over Meru, former warrior-turned-diggers reached to unmarried girls for comfort.

The traditions governing sexual relations between warriors and unmarried women died as well. Before the conquest, warriors gladly accepted over a decade of sexual abstinence, believing it maximized courage and strength. Male-female contact, whether physical or vocal, was forbidden.

After weapons were banned, however, warriors everywhere turned to the Gikuyu sexual custom of *ngweko* (KiMeru: nguiko). This allowed an unmarried woman to tuck a leather "pubic apron" between her legs and across her vagina. It was tied with many knots and could never be raised. Men who even attempted this were both whipped by *askaris* and automatically cursed by the always-watching ancestors. Thus protected, a woman could lie with and fondle her partner, receiving his caresses in turn. Thus, a warrior could relieve his physical needs without impregnating his partner.

Sadly, the *nguiko* system, too, was buried by corruption. Gikuyu porters, immune from punishment by either Horne's *askari* or (Meru) ancestral curses, began to compel Meru girls to perform *nguiko* with them every night. Meru chiefs and *askari* were quick to follow, and the demoralized warrior rank-and-file soon did the same. The girls, equally saddened by the total demoralization of the young men, proved unable to resist the attractions of drink, drunkenness, limited sex, and ultimately full intercourse.

One result was a Meru-wide explosion of abortions, on a scale never before imagined. Traditional midwives, attempting to end early pregnancies, were imprisoned by over-enthusiastic chiefs, desperate to follow Horne's increasingly frantic anti-abortion orders. Fathers seeking midwives for their daughters were accused of witchcraft and fined.

The alternative, of course, in areas where anti-abortion campaigns were successful, was a second explosion of fatherless children. The warrior fathers, unable to raid, seize cattle, and thus acquire bride wealth, were unable to marry and thus provide the children with families. In time, abandoned children would appear—a status unimagined by prior Meru generations—to be gathered in by the first Christian missionaries. In time, some of the unmarried girls would turn to prostitution—again to be taken in by missions. However, neither of these tragedies equaled the sadness endured by the men of Murungi age-set—the last generation of joyous, proud cattle raiding warriors—for whom everything that had made their lives worthwhile had died with the coming of England.

Chapter 10
"God" Comes to Meru

The White man's God first reached Meru in 1909, one
year after Horne completed his bloodless conquest of the
entire region. The idea was carried to Meru with Rev. John
B. Griffths, a British Methodist Minister with years of
experience on the Kenya Coast. Griffiths was inspired by
both the rapid British conquest of Embu (1906) and Horne's
bloodless seizure of Meru in 1907–8. Griffith petitioned the
Colonial government, asking them to grant "all Meru" to his
United Methodist Church. Receiving permission, he walked,
with one European companion and 24 Gikuyu porters, 171
miles around Mt. Kenya's entire eastern slope.

He arrived at "Fort Meru" in 1909, to find himself warmly
welcomed by Horne. Advising him not to penetrate deeper
into the "still quite savage" Meru country, Horne offered both
continuous social contact and swift military protection by
allotting the Methodists a plot of land less than two miles
from his headquarters.

Griffith's subsequent report back to London electrified
Methodist leaders:

*"It is a land of hills, valleys and innumerable streams…unlike
any other area in Africa…covered with ferns… thick with
blackberries…and mosquitos are unknown…Sirs, here it is.
The future of our East African Mission lies here."*

Methodist leaders began searching for both a minister and doctor. They offered both positions to Rev. Reginald Worthington, who sailed for Kenya in 1912, joining Griffiths in Mombasa. Then, they travelled the same 171 miles by foot, circling Mt. Kenya's Eastern slope until reaching Horne in Imenti.

Horne was delighted. He had chosen a cool, pleasant site, near both flowing water and an unending forest that could be used for wood. Unfortunately, the land was already the property of an Imenti clan. Horne offered to buy it, paying in cows. The elders wanted no further Whites living near them, least of all on their clan lands.

To rid themselves of both Griffiths and Worthington, they counter-offered land in a "sacred" forest glade reserved to the *nkoma*. In theory, no Meru dared enter. In practice, the grove was used by *kiamas* of curse-removers, who moved among the great trees gathering objects for their rituals. At night, they gathered to sing. All other Meru believed that the distant singing, heard faintly through the darkness, came from the Ancestral Spirits.

Horne knew this grove as a forest of "witchdoctors." The elders knew that if Whites harmed the sacred forest, the *nkoma* would wreak traditional revenge. Griffiths and Worthington knew, however, that "a forest of witches and wizards" was the most fitting place in Meru to sow the seed of God. The agreement was made. The cattle were transferred from Horne to the land-owning clan. A third log cabin was erected, this one for Worthington, as Griffith returned to the

Coast. The elders waited in vain for the *nkoma* to strike. None did. Finally, the work of spreading God could begin.

Italian Catholic Missionaries

Catholic Missionaries in Kenya had also grown interested in Horne's bloodless conquest of what they decided were the peaceful people of Meru. In 1910, two Catholic priests set off to explore the Meru region. Making the long trek around Mt. Kenya, they reached Horne at Fort Meru, intending to establish their mission next to his base.

Horne was not pleased. As an English member of the Anglican Church, he had little use for either Catholics or Italians, particularly those who spoke no English. Speaking in Gikuyu (through the Italians' Gikuyu porters), Horne informed the priests of a rule that required all mission stations to be at least ten miles apart. Since the Methodists already resided near Horne, the Italians would have to go south. Since Imenti was ten miles wide, the Italians would have to go beyond it, find what they could, buy it on their own, and survive.

They did not do well. Moving not only south but downhill, they eventually chose to found their mission on a flat, marshy plain that bordered both lower Imenti and Tharaka. It was a bad choice.

"The dry season heat never stops. The wet season rains never stop. The marshes breed mosquitos in unending clouds, often so thick as to impair breathing (at a time when the cause of Malaria was

unknown). Most important, few Africans live in this mosquito-ridden marsh. Thus, there is no one to convert."

Both men fell ill, again and again, with what was then known as "the fevers" (malaria), and the site was eventually abandoned.

Two other Italian priests then selected a site higher up the mountain, near today's Igoji Town. They then returned to Fort Meru, asking Horne's aid in buying the land from its Igoji owners. Horne unenthusiastically agreed. However, whatever number of goats the Italians offered was flatly rejected by all of the owners, with the obvious approval of 50 or so onlookers. The watchers understood that the initial refusal was merely the required prelude to a long and pleasant period of negotiation. Whatever number of goats the Italians offered would have to be divided (and subdivided) both among the many original owners of the plot, but all of their tenants. Deciding who was eligible for what part of which goat would take weeks. To flatly refuse an initial offer was simply required politeness.

Horne, however, had no knowledge whatsoever of Meru commercial traditions and no patience at all with the time they consumed. Unexpectedly, he cut through the rising babble of increasingly angry voices by striking the spokesman of the land-owning group to the ground. Dead silence followed. Stunned and frightened, the spokesman agreed immediately to the priest's original terms. A deeper reason for the acceptance, however, lay in the unspoken desire of the entire Igoji community to acquire "White men of their own," to protect them from the rising power of those northern Imenti clans who had "possession" of Horne.

Church of Scotland Missionaries

World War I halted all missionary expansion. In 1919, however, a single Scotsman, Earnest Carr, electrified the Kenya branch of the Church of Scotland by offering sufficient funds to launch a five-year missionary effort in Mwimbi, Muthambe, and Chuka. As WWI ended, Carr's daughter married Dr. A. Clive Irvine, an evangelical and medical missionary who had received British degrees in both the arts and medicine.

During WWI, Irvine had worked as a British medical officer, becoming fluent in what was then known as "native medicine," as well as both Swahili and Gikuyu. On leaving the Army, Irvine learned that Carr had offered the astounding sum of 1,000 pounds per year for the first five years of the mission station's life.

"These funds must be used to survey and select a suitable site and then construct a home, hospital, school, and carpenter's workshop. Electricity and running water will also be funded as they become available."

In short, it was to be a missionary's dream mission. Irvine and his new wife accepted the offer within hours. The agreement stipulated that they had to remain at the post for five years. Carr, having settled the financing, joined another senior missionary to trek around Mt. Kenya and select a site. On reaching Mwimbi, they were met by Mbogore wa Mwendo, once a notable war leader and now an Upper Mwimbe Blanket Chief.

Mbogore was a man of huge stature and great intelligence. As a younger warrior, before the arrival of English, he had wandered into the territory of several neighboring tribes—always displaying the symbols of peace. From his hosts, he had learned all the rumors of the oncoming Whites, growing increasingly concerned. Returning home, he was horrified to learn of the sheer savagery displayed by the Whites in their defeat of Embu.

Deciding to see for himself, he walked into Embu, protected by kinsmen, and was guided to Horne himself—at that time one of the three Englishmen directing the attack. Oddly, they got on well. Horne, as a man of small stature, admired both Mbogore's muscular frame and unusual height. On impulse, he gave the war leader Meru's first black blanket and proclaimed him "chief" of his Mwimbi people. Although unable to fathom the concept of "chief," Mbogore clearly grasped the extent of European military superiority. Thus, returned to his own people determined to persuade them to accept the British in peace.

As Horne's first black-blanket chief, Mbogore profited hugely from the conquest. Immediately grasping the unprecedented extent of his new power, Mbogore used it to increase the number of his sheep, goats, cows, and wives. In consequence, he became a devoted ally of both Horne and "Kingi Georgi," who symbolized Great Britain.

Mbogore therefore met the two Scottish missionaries with considerable joy. He urged them to construct a mission station just next to his hut, where he could both control and enrich himself from their activities. Carr, fully understanding what the war leader wanted, eventually chose a site near what was becoming The Great Horne Road. More important, it was not only near a flowing river, but adjacent to a striking waterfall that could provide both irrigation and electricity.

The Whites were jubilant. Mbogore was appalled. Nonetheless, he submitted to their instructions to use his blanket *askaris* to round up wood-cutters across Mwimbi. These were set to work, often under the whip, cutting huge trees and reshaping them into simple bridges across the racing rivers.

Soon after the bridges were complete, a massive caravan of 74 carts arrived, each hauled painfully across the slippery, creaking bridges by teams of oxen. The carts carried whatever was needed to construct a house, hospital, school, sheds, and whatever else the Irvines might require.

Clive Irvine arrived some months later, in a single-ox wagon, carrying his wife and a newborn son. He plunged into his work with enormous enthusiasm, asking Mbogore to have *askari* comb the villages for workers. The buildings went up quickly, but they felt empty. The mission station looked substantial, but in the beginning, no one came.

Chapter 11

Spreading God

The search for converts began as soon as the buildings were completed. Methodist, Catholics, and Church of Scotland missionaries alike faced the problem of spreading God's word among peoples thoroughly content with their own religious system. For Methodists, the problem was compounded by their own beliefs about African religion:

"No tribe in Kenya is more deeply steeped in witchcraft than the Ameru. Witchcraft is their religion and the wizard their high priest."

Missionaries of all three faiths were equally blinded by the beliefs they held about European witchcraft. At that time, all three religions defined it as the use of supernatural powers solely to cause harm, whether to crops, flocks, or people. These powers were derived from the devil, a supernatural being created by God explicitly to harm others. The harm was done by casting spells (curses) that hurt, damaged, sickened, or killed the intended victims. The European witchcraft system stopped there. Their only remedy was to burn the alleged practitioners—almost always women—thus destroying their abilities to curse and thus harm others.

Europeans were both intellectually and psychologically incapable of grasping the comparative complexity of the African system, in which the curse was used as a psychological tool to resolve the conflicts inevitable between human beings, and thereby retain social peace. The rituals used to curse, remove a curse, detect a curser, and reconcile that curser and his victim were all clumped together in the missionary's minds as evil acts (witchcraft) committed by evil people (witchdoctors), whose only possible purpose was to cause evil.

Methodist Missionaries: Stories, Sugar, Salt, and Ndinguri

Only the Methodist's Reverend Worthington began to investigate the system. His mission's directors in London had asked him to

"engage in constant study of the evils particular to this country (Meru), so as to devise ways to combat them."

After many discussions with nearby elders, Worthington concluded that the Meru did believe in a Supreme Being, named Murungu. He lived atop Mt. Kenya but was either indifferent or hostile to the people below. Murungu, it was believed, was responsible for acts such as withholding rain or sending locusts. Good fortune, in contrast, simply meant he had turned his attention elsewhere.

Ignored by God, Worthington decided, the people had turned to the worship of spirits. Some were spirts of the forests, living within waterfalls, rivers, or huge old trees. Others were ancestors, the spirits of those who had recently died. All of them needed to be placated by near continuous sacrifice of livestock. All were believed to be capable of anger, striking out against individual Meru with deadly curses.

In consequence, daily life was lived in constant fear. Worthington thus perceived Meru religion as a "religion of fear." The idea of a God who only loved his people—all his people—was beyond the range of Meru thought.

Worthington's first act against what he perceived as the "forces of darkness" came from his need to cut firewood. Without thinking, he asked his cook to cut some from the adjacent forest. The cook refused, as did every other man he asked. Asking why, he learned what the Imenti elders had always known when they allowed him to settle; that his mission had been set adjacent to a scared grove.

Worthington's first response was to cut the wood himself, day after day. The local elders, stunned that he did not sicken and die, decided that the *nkoma* had fled before the evil in the iron of his ax.

His next step was simply to go walking. He would enter a village, approach a group of elders, and, using a Gikuyu translator, begin telling them stories of Jesus.

He called this tactic "extensive preaching." It did not work well. Many listeners simply lost interest and wandered off. Stories told in the heat of the dry season put listeners to sleep; stories in the rainy season led listeners to seek shelter.

Worthington did not know, of course, that he was violating a Meru tradition. There was a time for tales, histories, songs, etc., but in the evening, after people who had worked all day, had eaten, and could sit near a fire and listen to the wisdom of elders. Worthington, of course, was no elder and thus—by Meru standards—not yet old enough to offer "wisdom" to those older than himself.

He then shifted to what he called "intensive preaching." This consisted of simply inviting elders over to his house. This tactic began well, until those visiting realized that the White man did not mean to provide them with millet beer—the traditional offering of any host to guests. Unfortunately, British Methodists of this era regarded beer drinking as a sin—one of the many forms of human behavior they meant to eradicate. Annoyed at what they perceived as his lack of traditional hospitality, the elders stayed away.

Worthington then switched to children, particularly *ndinguri* (older boys between 11–15), inviting them to sit near his doorway, then bribing them with stories, sugar, salt, and strips of cloth. Since boys this age traditionally went naked, the cloth was prized as symbolic of their approaching adulthood.

However, the stories soon proved to be the greatest attraction. As Worthington's mastery of KiMeru (Meru language) improved, he became an artful story teller, holding ever-larger groups of *ndinguri* spellbound. A few, moreover, gradually became addicted to reading. Several of these would grow up to become Meru's first Methodist converts.

Catholic Missionaries: Walking, Greetings, and Snuff

In contrast, the Catholic fathers relied on walking everywhere to spread the word of God. Initially, this word was in Gikuyu, since the Italian fathers spoke neither KiMeru nor English. Translators were found among Gikuyu boys who had been orphaned, then placed in a Catholic orphanage in the Gikuyu region. They had all learned some Italian, thus quickly proved able to translate between that language and KiMeru.

The priests' first tactic, therefore, was to visit the surrounding homesteads and give gifts.

"We began Christ's work by giving greetings and tobacco, salt, or snuff."

This fell squarely within Meru traditions of hospitality, which required visitors to a homestead to present gifts to its head, receiving gifts from him in return. The exchange was intended to create good feelings on both sides, eventually leading them to become friends.

Homesteads receiving visits required their wives to brew huge gourds of millet beer on days when the strangers were expected. The priests shared it gladly, then invited the homestead elders to visit them in turn—again precisely following Meru tradition. On days when elders appeared, the priests hired women who lived near them to brew beer for the guests. Thus, each Sunday found the tiny mission station awash with visitors, all drinking and exchanging stories, which gave the priests a first chance to speak of Jesus.

The Italians gradually extended their visits outwards from the mission station. On occasion, they took on darker tasks, allowing the priests to move beyond their intial role as guests. For example, if a priest entered a home where an occupant lay ill, he followed his own tradition and dispensed such medicine as he carried, while refusing to accept anything in return. This, of course, violated Meru tradition, which called for gifts to be exchanged for gifts. Those who gave "medicine" without receiving gifts in return were believed to be *arogi*, or cursers. One priest, who refused all gifts offered him as payment, was eventually denounced as a curser and his medicines were constantly refused.

If a priest entered a hut in which the occupant was dying, he again followed his own tradition and administered the last rites. When asked what he was doing, the reply was that he was "cleansing" the dying person's spirit to prepare it for God. Meru listeners, well pleased, translated "cleansing" as "curse removal," one pillar of their own religious belief. Thus, a priest was always welcomed by the dying, and pleased in his turn to have "reclaimed a soul."

Church of Scotland: Pig Wars, Medicines, and Prayer

Dr. Clive Irvine plunged into his religious work with untiring enthusiasm. His first attempt to befriend his Mwimbi neighbors took the form of a war against wild pigs. These lived in hordes along the forest fringes, foraying out each night to graze on growing millet. The owners fought them with slings, stones, and spears, but were gradually losing the war. Irvine poisoned entire herds using strychnine brought in from Nairobi, an act of war that made him many friends.

He then turned to spreading Christ through Western medicine. He was fortunate in that one particularly visible disease was spreading rapidly throughout Meru. The British called it "yaws," a condition in which the legs and lower body become covered with visible sores.

By 1920, a treatment for yaws became available in Kenya. Armed with vast quantities of the compound, Irvine then began to challenge local healers (whom he regarded as witchdoctors), to compete with him in treating yaws. He always won, thus gaining an unintended but region-wide reputation as a curse-remover.

He then waged a second war, this one on the concept of *mugiro*. As a doctor, he often asked his Mwimbi patients what they believed had caused their ills. As a missionary, he grew angry when every patient asserted that every form of illness was the result of a curse that had been ritually placed on the sufferer, either by an enemy or spirit—angered by the patient's violation of a taboo.

Irvine argued that faith in Christ was like a shield, protecting believers from any curse hurled at them, whether by enemies, forest spirits, or Mwimbi ancestors.

"To raise that shield, we had only to pray directly to Jesus, displaying one's faith in him both with lips and heart."

To dramatize his point, he led a few fearful *ndinguri* into the fringes of a sacred grove. A pond lay within the grove. The spring that fed it flowed between two rocks. Mwimbi tradition held that the ancestral sprits had entered the grove between the rocks. Irvine blocked the flow, thereby symbolically locking the *nkoma* into the ground. He then invited the *ndinguri* in his party to join him in gathering branches for that night's firewood.

Once more, the elders awaited ancestral retribution. None came. Each day that illness or calamity did not strike, Irvine led a small but growing group of youths in mass prayers of thanksgiving, assuring them that lifelong faith would lead to lifelong protection and beyond it, into heaven. As belicf in the new faith took root, the converts themselves entered sacred groves on every ridgetop, cutting first the branches and then the ancient trees. In so doing, they killed not only portions of their own protective forest but a beloved tradition that went back to the origin of their people.

These same converts also turned on the traditional ritualists. Ignoring their actual ritual specialties (curse placement, curse removal, curse detection, etc.), they denounced them all as witchdoctors, borrowing the non-African term from Irvine. Groups of them invaded the elders' huts at sundown, chanting, mocking, and often physically chasing them into the adjacent forest. Worse, they seized the goat-skin bags in which the ritualists held their medicines, carefully preserved in antelope horns. These they burned or threw into nearby rivers.

Their "Christian" goal was to stop people from visiting all specialists in ritual to deal with curses. The actual result was to deprive these elderly men of their livelihood, depriving them of the gifts of honey-beer, millet, and goats on which they subsisted. Over time, a traditional form of social security, which had protected the aged for generations, shriveled away. As the direct result of Christian persecution, many elders began to starve.

The Lure of Reading

It was not only the new beliefs that drew *ndinguri* to Irvine; it was the new learning. Those who came to the mission were required to participate in twice-daily prayers, at dawn and dusk. The evening prayer sessions were then extended into instruction. The initial stories of Jesus became biblical tales. This was broadened in turn to become an introduction to reading. Some few of the older boys were thrilled, first with the idea that a book could tell stories and then that *they* could tell stories by making marks on a paper.

Over time, adults also joined all three of the Christian faiths. Some were ill and sought the shield of Jesus alongside their medicine. Others were half-castes; boys or men whose fathers had come from other tribes and who had thus been exposed to other beliefs. A few were potential outcasts, cattle owners whose herds had been seized by a corrupt chief and who came in hope that a missionary might appeal the seizure to Horne. If they succeeded, some stayed with the Church, shielded from that chief's retribution by the power of prayer.

In general, the three Christian groups initially evolved into a new and unprecedented form of fringe *kiama*, no different than those the *aathi* hunters or the dancing deviants of *mwaa*. Frozen out of mainstream society, they could find comfort and companionship only among themselves.

Chapter 12
The War Against Converts

Not once did the elders of any Meru region act in defense of their religious traditions. Not once did any elder's *kiama* speak out against the new faith, even when the sacred groves were desecrated or their ritualists abused. Instead they used a weapon sanctified by centuries of tribal tradition: ostracism. For generations, men of the Meru mainstream had responded to social deviation by ostracizing the deviants. By refusing to share tribal rituals with men of the fringe, a *kiama* of ruling elders could deny them existence within mainstream society.

Total Exclusion

Social exclusion had been used against the hunters and ironsmiths on the Meru migration and had been successfully extended against each new form of deviation that had appeared. In consequence, all deviant *kiamas* remained on society's fringe. This new *kristo-kiama*, in all its forms, would be no different. The elders were content.

Their sons, the family-heads, were not. Their anger was directed against the creation of schools. Tradition permitted Meru children to sing, chant, and listen to stories, but only after their chores were done and the sun was down. Their days were spent tending the family flocks and herds.

European tradition, in contrast, required "work" (here, schooling) in daylight, especially after children began to read. The issue was not one of faith but use of time. Irvine saw constant school attendance as a path out of what he perceived as "savagery." School absenteeism was forbidden. The family heads saw it as a social deviation; children who refused to work for the family were labeled deviant, thus subject to ostracism.

"I myself would have gone to school were it not for those people who were laughing at others who did. Everyone was laughing at the wasomaji (readers), insulting them, calling them names and singing songs against them. In fact, at first, I was among those who sang the songs."

This behavior often frightened the converts' mothers, who would appear at the "school" (actually a boys' *gaaru*, or war-barrack) and beg their sons to give up this madness and return home. This became particularly intense if a boy was sick. One mother, terrified when her son grew ill but refused to turn home, appeared at the school to plead:

"My son, how can you wait for death in a house of sickness, when you can come home to a muga (curse remover) and be made well?"

The boys' fathers took more direct action. Some simply walked into the school, disrupting lessons, to seize their sons "by a wrist or an ear" and drag them away. Others sent their older sons, now warriors, to stand by the school in silence, their very presence intimidating every boy within to leave. Other fathers publicly expelled their convert sons from the family with curses, kicks, and beatings.

*"My father cursed me as a 'mwiji' (small boy, a deadly insult),
shouting that he had many cows that I could tend instead of lying idle
like a child and hearing endless tales."*

Converts treated in this fashion lost all contact not only with their kin but every age-mate. The loss, traumatic within any society, was terrifying in a communal setting and one that sent them swiftly into the Christian embrace.

It was made worse when the missionaries decided that every Christian boy must publicly display his devotion to Jesus by cutting their hair in European fashion. This meant shaving off the red-clay-colored warrior braid, a mark of boyhood pride from childhood. Wearing the braid symbolized a boy's desire to become both a warrior and a man. Cutting it off symbolically emasculated him, its loss instantly identifying him as a *mwiji* who wished to neither become warrior or man. That left every one of them subject to constant taunts, thrown rocks, and frequent beatings, both by other boys and entire groups of warriors.

The Warriors' War on Converts

It was the warriors, however, who spearheaded resistance against the converts. Their hostility was based on two fears. One was that *ndinguri* might join the Church instead of becoming warriors. The second was the pleasure they expected from "training" the older boys—invariably by collectively beating them—into complete obedience.

Initially, no warrior band used force. Instead, if Christian *ndinguri* walked anywhere they were met by warrior taunt-songs, intended to publicly display their lack of manhood to every unmarried girl in the community. Consider the impact the "song of the striped mouse" must have had on 11–15-year-old boys, newly shamed by the compulsory shaving of their beautiful and much-prized warrior braids:

"Who is this hairless animal? Who is this fearful animal? It is the mission mwiji. Your little heads are shaved (in stripes), so that you look like a striped mouse. Why do you wear women's (Western) clothes like mission fools? Why do you dance (in Western ways) like mission fools? Are you the mission Mwiji?"

Other warrior bands displayed their antagonism through dance. Aware of the Christian distaste for nakedness, warrior bands from several ridgetops initiated what the missionaries subsequently called "dirty dancing," but the warriors knew as the traditional *authi*. Warriors would gather at night on what was once their dancing field, but now held the school boys' imitation *gaaru*.

The warriors began by chanting. One by one, they carried out a magnificent *authi*, each bounding, naked, across the dancing field to within inches of the school door. There they would shout out new versions of the traditional battle vows. Whereas, before the conquest, they had vowed to seize whole herds or not come back, now they vowed to seize every *ndinguri* in the school or never leave the dancing field. The boys—and missionaries—were properly terrified. However, on completing their dance the warriors returned to their *gaaru.* Under colonial law, such seizure was forbidden. Thus, there was nothing more they could do.

Warrior bands also played what the missionaries called "tricks" on the converts. In fact, they were savage attempts to make it impossible for mission boys to ever leave their mission. One example was for warriors to wait until an entire group of converts had knelt to loudly pray. Having learned that a prayer must be completed before the boys could rise, the warriors would pounce on every member of the group and slash their western clothes.

Another tactic was to wait until a convert, having returned home, followed family tradition and led the goats out to graze. Again, the warriors would pounce, this time on the flock, chasing all of them in different directions into the bush. Their goal was to teach every convert that he could no longer participate in normal Meru life.

A more serious conflict emerged when *ndinguri* converts deliberately violated those warrior traditions that concerned themselves. As older boys, custom required them to publicly acknowledge warrior superiority each time they passed each other on a path. The *ndinguri* were not only required to give way but throw themselves into hiding in the bush, peeping up from the ground as the warriors passed. This practice not only cleared the paths in times of war but reinforced warrior status in the minds of those who would one day become warriors.

Unfortunately, Rev. Worthington decided to send his little band of converts on onto the public paths each Sunday, specifically to stop passing warriors—even blocking their way—and pray to them to come to church. Worthington acted from a normal English, Christian perspective. The boys, however, were caught between conflicting traditions. The warriors, seeing only the violation of their cherished custom, beat every boy with the flat of their swords, then sent them running back to what rapidly became their only place of safety—for the next Sunday Worthington would order the boys onto the paths and the conflict would play itself out again.

Treating Converts as Arogi (Cursers)

Only once did this *ndinguri-nthaka* (older boy-warrior) hostility rise to the level of hatred and death. It began when one group of schoolers began to play soccer on what had always been a warrior dancing ground. When the warriors appeared, commanding them to leave, the converts refused.

Stunned and furious, but legally unable to use force, the warriors decided that every one of the converts (now, 11 boys) should be seized and immediately circumcised, thereby transforming them into warriors who could be welcomed into their ranks. Their intent was entirely benevolent; an attempt to permanently end the conflict by reminding the boys that the moment had come to abandon the boyhood foolishness that had led them into foreign ways.

Unfortunately, the first step in the circumcision process was to humble the prospective candidates by requiring them to brew many large gourds of millet beer, then deliver them to the warrior *gaaru*. The brewing process was long, repetitive, dull, and—as a result—was considered the work of women. The converts, hating the idea, appealed to Worthington. The missionary had no idea that brewing was the first step toward warriorhood. He did know, however, that all Methodists everywhere were forbidden all forms of alcohol as sinful. He forbade the boys to brew; the converts passed that order on to the warriors and refused outright.

The warriors, forbidden by their own traditions to drink the beer once it had been delivered, would simply have passed it on to their fathers. However, if the *ndinguri* refused to brew it, they were rejecting warriorhood itself. The warriors, staggered by the enormity of their refusal, took the only route tradition still allowed. They decided that every one of the boys had become *arogi* (cursers) and thus a danger to the community. In consequence, the boys were to be given the punishment reserved for cursers; they were to be wrapped in banana leaves and burned.

Knowing none of this, Worthington left Meru for Nairobi. Emboldened by his absence, members of the warrior band appeared at the boys' school dormitory, built of wooden poles, papyrus reeds, and dry banana leaves to resemble a warrior *gaaru*. At 4 a.m., the traditional time for a raid, they silently piled wood across the only door, blocking it shut. Then they set the pile afire.

The 11 converts were asleep. The wind whipped up the blaze so that it spread instantaneously along the roof and walls. As the boys woke, it must have seemed as if the entire hut was afire. Some boys groped blindly at the door, then threw themselves against it. It did not move. Then, the wooden poles, themselves alight, began to fall down on the heads and shoulders of the screaming boys, burning them once more as they rolled underfoot. Smoke-blind and terrified, they were incapable of a single unified actin, such as charging through the *gaaru* at a single point:

"We were like frightened buffalo, charging and stumbling against one another as each shouted out what the other should do."

Finally, the fire itself consumed so much fuel that a hole appeared. One boy charged it—and burst through. The others followed, all screaming with the pain of their burns. The warriors melted away as the boys raced barefoot through the darkness to the hut of the Mission's only other European, Frank Mimmack, an English carpenter. Although deeply shaken and fearful of an attack on the mission itself, Mimmack treated the boys' burns—but five of them died. Horne, of course, began an immediate investigation, but was met by a wall of silence.

Imenti elders felt that the warriors had acted solely to preserve tradition. The behavior of converts, corrupted through their contact with White men, had become so deviant that it endangered the very framework of the social order. Tradition permitted the execution of such deviants, relabeling them as *arogi* (cursers) who used their powers beyond the capacity of society to bear. In consequence, the guilty went unpunished so that warriorhood might survive.

The Christian Islands

In the face of such hostility, Catholic, Methodist, and Church of Scotland missionaries alike realized that to survive their flocks must become Christian islands, living in isolation from the surrounding hostile tribal sea. This was a sharp departure from earlier ideals, when Christian missionaries everywhere saw themselves embracing all of Africa with open arms. Instead, beset with similar problems, they used the European boarding school model to shield their followers from harassment, temptation, and the loneliness that came from leaving age-mates, kinsmen, and parents behind.

"It was the greatest disobedience. To tell that I was going to join the Christians crushed my age-mates, family and parents. To my clan, I was dead. To my kin, I was dead. To my parents, I was dead."

The missionaries, however, knew the converts were not "dead," since they could always return. To prevent this, they recreated the lifestyle of the English Boarding schools, as places into which converts could retreat and live a peaceful, Christian life.

However, there was no peace. Each night, the darkness filled with the sounds of the warriors, singing songs that either mocked the converts' manhood or begged them to reclaim it, simply by rejoining their age-mates in the dancing that would transform them once more into comrades in arms.

Chapter 13

The Choice: Anglicization or Supression

By the 1920s, the goals of British Colonialism had shifted sharply. In the first years of conquest, pioneering tribal district officers took both pleasure and pride in learning everything they could about those they now ruled. Horne, for example, stayed in Meru from 1907–17—a decade that formed only part of a long colonial career. He learned KiMeru, Gikuyu, Embu and four other African languages. Horne's method of learning tribal secrets was to ask the elders. He often did not grasp the complexities of what he was told. Nonetheless he—and those Whites who served with him—began to understand the lives of Africans.

That changed. WWI had decimated the ranks of colonial officials. Consecutive epidemics and droughts decimated the Meru, thereby doubling the administrative measures required to keep people alive. One major result was a change in the type of Colonial Administrator that now ruled. Whereas the pioneers had sought tribal knowledge, the new men saw themselves as efficiency experts. Collectively, they had neither the time, language, skills, nor human curiosity to probe deeply and searchingly into tribal knowledge, which they perceived as tribal secrets.

Instead, their professional pride lay in administrative efficiency, which they defined as the ability to force Africans to get tasks done. Thus, huts were to be counted in record time, taxes collected in record amounts, labor recruited in record numbers. British standards of law, religion, morality, and civilized behavior were going to be imposed with record speed. Above all, in exchange for this introduction to English ("civilized") behavior, England's colonial subjects were to be taught how to show a profit.

Unfortunately, those levels of administrative efficiency relied on interpreters—who were Gikuyu. Few Meru learned Swahili (the colonial *lingua franca*) and almost no Meru learned English. No Gikuyu loved the Meru. All of them felt they were forced to live among savages. They identified wholly with England and believed themselves above the peoples they now helped rule. Consider the story of a Kikuyu interpreter for Horne, Salimu the Small:

"To see the White man (Horne), Salimu asked a goat. To argue your case before him, Salimu asked a girl. If you complained, he asked his White man to put you in prison."

The interpreters "reinterpreted" the Meru world as they wanted their British superiors to view it. They left no stone unturned to convince their employers that every tribal social institution was primitive, savage, and dangerous.

Often those descriptions corresponded precisely with what the newly appointed district officers wanted to hear:

"I am told that my natives are sunk in superstition and abominable practices...(and remain) backward due to their belief in witchcraft and curses."

Small wonder that the once-extensive colonial knowledge of Meru lifestyles completely disappeared. It was replaced by a rising desire, shared by every colonial officer, to anglicize and thereby civilize the Empire's subject peoples.

Anglicizing Njuri Nceki

The most memorable example of this were the tactics used by these colonial officers against the *njuri nceki*, the most senior council of Meru elders, with branches in both Imenti-Igoji and Tigania-Igembe.

One tactic was to anglicize all branches of the *njuri nceki*, transforming them eventually into English-style committees. Having learned what he could about the *njuri's* existence, the first District Commissioner (DC) to attempt this proclaimed a "General *kiama* for all Meru," inviting the *njuri* elders from all four sections to meet at his headquarters. Dutifully, the many elders walked the required many miles to appear.

On arriving, they sat, awaiting the new DC's arrival. Initially, they were offended to learn that he had provided no millet beer—always the prerequisite of every social gathering. Then, they were angered to learn that the meeting was to be conducted by men younger than themselves, again a particularly insulting violation of tradition. Finally, they were enraged to be told that each decision would be made that afternoon by majority vote, ignoring the entire Meru decision-making process, which required days of meat, beer, debate, and gradual consensus. Quietly deciding that no *kiama* had, in fact, been convened all the elders vanished. So did the plan to anglicize *njuri*.

Suppressing Njuri Nceki

The second tactic was to replace *njuri* altogether, banning its meetings, burning its huts, and transferring its functions to British-educated youngsters. The DC that most strongly advocated this appeared in the early 1920s. The only name by which he is remembered, by the Meru, is *Kivunja*. The destroyer.

Kivunja saw the *njuri* as powerful but reactionary, dragging its people backward into a witch-ridden past. By using curses to enforce their demands, these "secret societies" could overawe all Meru, thereby paralyzing each British effort to improve their lives.

His first objection was to the *njuri* practice of feasting—consuming the bulls brought to the elders as gifts to repay and thank those who resolved their conflicts. Meru tradition sanctified such feasting as symbolic proof that a conflict had been resolved.

Unaware of the symbolic context in which each feast took place, Kivunja condemned all elders for "taking bribes" and "wasting meat." He then banned *njuri* throughout Meru, enforcing the decision by burning several of their huts. The ban proved effective. The Igoji and Imenti *njuris* no longer met. The Igembe and Tigangia councils initially tried to ignore the ban but found "informers too many and police too near." Over time, subsequent DCs grew uncertain that that *njuri nceki* existed. What they were told is that it was nothing more than one of the many small secret witchcraft societies to be found everywhere in Meru.

In time British colonizers merely followed the tactics used by earlier conquerors through history. In theory, they were simply training Meru to rule themselves in British fashion, thereby freeing them from living lives of fear under what they perceived as African savagery. In fact, they were eliminating every indigenous institution, then filling the void with their own. This was achieved by training the young to assume the leadership positions of the old. Beholden solely to the conquerors for their power, this new generation would simply follow English orders, thereby eroding the old ways and transforming British rule into reality.

Rumors of Witchcraft

By the mid 1920s every colonial institution in Meru was grinding to a halt. Local Native Councils, established by various DCs and staffed with native Christians, passed fewer and fewer laws—all ignored by everyone. Local Native Tribunals, also British-sponsored and staffed, resolved no cases, since no people appeared to ask for justice. In short, every British-sponsored form of Meru government was universally ignored.

Initially, DCs attributed this situation to sullenness, backwardness, passive resistance, and delight in abominable practices. The Meru became notable in Colonial circles as "difficult, backward, steeped in witchcraft" and thus, an unpopular people with whom to work.

Over time, however, administrators began to feel that Meru non-cooperation might have a deeper cause—which they eventually decided was witchcraft. By the mid 1920s, Meru district officers believed they knew a great deal about Meru witchcraft. They divided practitioners into three types: One was the "witchdoctor," a term meant to include every significant form of Meru ritualist. Witchdoctors were old men who carried goat skin bags of evil medicines for use in cursing anyone who angered them at any time.

A second type was the "witchcraft band." The British saw these as groups of witchdoctors who had banded together to terrorize surrounding Meru into providing them with sex and food. They achieved this by threatening both the elders and family-heads with curses, collectively chanted so as to maximize the listener's terror.

"They have a huge hut in each of their locations to which they call a lot of young girls…who were not allowed to return to their parents…at night they held dances naked and had sexual intercourse.

"Aathi is the name of a secret society…we know it exists, but it is impossible to find out what things they do. They build large huts and stay in there and eat and drink and do worse things.

"The natives here are sunk in superstition…and abominable practices. Njuricheke Kiama (sic) is credited with supernatural power."

The third type, about which even less was known, were the "witchcraft tribunals," referring, of course, to *njuri nceki*.

"These were groups of elders operating in total secrecy.
No Meru would even speak of them to a District official. They met
at night, in huts they would build at sundown. They began a huge
fire, then compelled Meru to bring them bulls to roast, which they
devoured whole. Men failing to provide a bull were cursed by every
elder in the group."

The English, of course, had no interest in comprehending the social context of these bull feasts; not did any Meru ever tell them. The man who brought a bull sought justice in a dispute. The elders who consumed it dispensed justice, drawn from their collective wisdom. The English, believing that only *they* could dispense justice, condemned the gift-bull, communal feasting, and resolving conflict, all as acts of witchcraft.

"Today (1925), the more educated (Meru) claim the Njoli (sic: Njuri)
must be abolished because it keeps the country in darkness."

The Whites were most annoyed by their inability to learn any facts at all about these secret societies. Lacking knowledge, they created their own myths, imagining the fringe groups to be both multiplying across Meru and joining together to oppose England.

One priest, Father G. Bondino, decided on direct action. He did know that *kagita* feasts within his area were always preceded by the pounding of great drums, which coughed and rumbled till dawn. One night, having darkened his face and hands, he dressed entirely in black and followed the drums into the darkness.

The drumming led him to an unusually large hut, built of poles and banana leaves. Creeping undetected to its side, he peered in through the leaves. He saw nothing; the interior was dark except for a fire. Nor could he pick single words out of the hum of conversation. Straining forward to hear more, he stumbled, falling heavily against the hut. Men poured from the doorway. He was seized.

Both sides were both horribly embarrassed and thoroughly angry; Bondino for having been caught spying and his captors for not knowing what to do with the priest they had captured. Bondino demanded entry into the hut. His captors, ignoring his command, threatened to curse him instantly if he did not leave.

The Priest, raising the golden cross he carried on his neck, declared that Jesus shielded him from their curses. He was answered by a torrent of shouts, threatening him with retreat or death. Suddenly fearful, he left as he had come. The next day, Catholics burned the hut and everything in it to the ground. No European ever repeated Bondino's attempt to unmask the society, and the mystery remained.

It seemed perfectly logical for the British to conclude that Meru witchdoctors would band together to fight back against the conquerors. Certainly, the British themselves, under the heel of invaders, would have banded together to push them off. They also quite understood the use of curses, intended to intimidate the entire population into joining the resistance. The correct colonial response, therefore, was to eliminate them, both individually and as groups, to clear the way for both Christianity and Empire.

Chapter 14
White War Against Witchcraft

District Commissioner Frank Lamb, when assigned to Meru in 1926, knew exactly what he needed to do:

"I have been engaged in the investigation of witchcraft...
In addition to the usual form of witchcraft, there exist...two secret societies in which witchcraft is used to extort property or enforce its orders."

Lamb came into a district in which no African colonial servant carried out British orders, unless by direct command. Rather, they moved sullenly through the motions. British-sponsored laws were passed but universally ignored. British sponsored Tribunals made legal decisions that were universally ignored. British administrative orders were obeyed, implemented, and then ignored to whatever degree proved possible.

Lamb was convinced that every Meru member of the colonial administration had been paralyzed by the fear of anti-British curses, launched by anti-British societies. This passivity had spread across the region. On his initial inspection tour, Lamb found virtually every British-appointed chief and headman either unable or unwilling to do anything at all. Many were constantly drunk—a signal that they lived in fear. All were obsessed with acquiring "protective magic," but refused to tell Lamb what it was against.

Lamb's initial conclusion:

"The witchdoctors, secret witchcraft societies and illegal (witchcraft) tribunals" had banded together—through the use of potent curses— to rob…the entire machinery of British Administration of all initiative."

In 1928, Lamb was joined by G.H. Hopkins as his Assistant District Commissioner. After his own initial investigation, Hopkins concluded that these secret societies used two types of curse to enforce their demands. One was the use of visual symbols, such as the reddened sticks of *aathi* and the vines of *kagita*. The other was verbal, including the use of huge drums, dirty dancing, rough songs and chanted curses. He argued that all of these groups used both the visual and verbal curses to compel total obedience, by:

"…predicting (promising) a disastrous end for any (Meru) individual who agrees to adopt a progressive innovation… declaiming that the same fate will befall all others who stray to the teachings of Europe."

Lamb and Hopkins decided to investigate the three most dangerous of these societies, to ensure their eventual destruction. They chose *njuri nceki*, *kagita* and *aathi*.

The "Secret Societies" Evolve: Njuri Nceki Underground

Neither the many ridgetop *kiamas* nor their regional *njuris* were "secret" to anyone in Meru. Tradition required, however, that they establish a total wall of silence against all

British inquiries. The *kiamas* did make adjustments. When the British burned their traditional gathering huts, they met in forest glades. If discovered and then accused of holding secret meetings, they argued that they had simply gathered to drink beer.

Quietly, they did what they had always done—gathering to resolve each instance of local conflict and ritual cursing. They accepted the bulls as traditional gifts. They resolved each local conflict in such fashion as to reconcile all sides. Finally, former enemies and current elders roasted and devoured the bulls, beyond the reach of District Officers. The sharing of meat symbolized that the conflict was resolved and social peace restored.

Kagita Underground

The many small *kiamas* of *kagita* had survived prior periods of famine by evolving into dancing societies. These became so successful that the various bands began to take root on the edges of mainstream communities. One group of dancers would build a huge hut and settle in. Their next step was to assure a predictable and plentiful supply of meat, beer, beans and millet.

To achieve this, they planted their traditional *ndindi* sticks along public paths, particularly those used by women to fetch water. If a woman saw a stick, she had been socialized since girlhood to believe she was cursed. Her only recourse—

as with men—was to go the *kagita* hut, offer the expected amounts of food and beer, and have the curse removed.

In this new era, however, a woman might also be "asked" (commanded) to join the dancers, both in their processions and at night in the hut. Beyond that, she might be required to "join" *kagita* itself, the obligation requiring her to provide daily portions of food.

"There was no choice for us unmarried girls. A kagita murogi (curser) would just point at you with his smallest finger and say 'you girl! Come into Kagita!'"

The forced inclusion of unwed girls had one unintended consequence—strangers often joined the dancing, bringing gifts of beer or goats. Often, they were lonely former warriors who wished to dance and thus forget the emptiness and lack of purpose in their lives. The single men, in turn, attracted single women who slipped away from their parents to combat their own despair, created by the sadness of their men.

Thus the 1920s saw steady *kagita* expansion. Existing *kiamas* grew, hived off, and multiplied, both by incorporating "victims" and offering refuge for the hungry, sexually deviant, depressed, and bored. The British and Italians raged at what they imagined was naked dancing, compulsory sex, and meat feasts as the result of extortion. Worse, they worried that the groups might band together, using their curses to persuade all Meru to rise up against the British Empire. In fact, *kiama kia kagita* remained what it had always been, a fringe society providing feasts, songs, and mild sexual deviations from the behavioral norms.

Aathi Underground

In contrast, the various *aathi kiamas* faced recurring catastrophe. Initially, both their hunting and honey zones were sufficiently protected by the planting of "bone" and "claw" *ndindi* sticks. Mainstream Meru largely respected these and stayed way. After the 1880s, however, non-Meru hunters (often with mainstream Meru partners) began to comb the lower forest fringes for elephants and tusks. The elephants moved uphill, deeper into the forests. The buffalo were hunted next, although many died through epidemics of rinderpest. As time passed, however, more mainstream Meru scavenged the lower forest. The *ndindi* sticks were increasingly ignored, and the honey-hives began to disappear.

Then, the real blow fell. Soon after the conquest, the Colonial Government restricted every Meru to his own ridgetop. To leave it, as previously mentioned, each man required a paper *chiti* (chit, identification pass) to be issued by his chief.

"Any "native" found outside his reserve (ridgetop) is subject to arrest."

The entire forest was declared reserved to the Crown. No Meru were to be allowed within. No hunting whatsoever was allowed. Evasion meant imprisonment. Every *aathi* lost his reason to exist.

Shattered, the various, small *aathi kiamas* migrated downhill. Like *kagita*, each group established a huge hut on the outer fringes of a mainstream settlement. Their first task was to protect it. The traditional "skull" was paced at the peak of each hut. *Ndindi* sticks, which had once protected hunting zones, now shielded the only place where *aathi* could still be themselves.

Again, like *kagita*, the next step was to insure a perpetual supply of beer and meat. Hunter tradition, of course, forbade the consumption of cattle and goats. Once again, those animals that *aathi* took from mainstream herders were renamed "bushbuck" and "buffalo." The *aathi* "hunt" also evolved. Since single hunters no longer had wildlife to stalk, their *kiamas* merely moved in procession through mainstream settlements, searching out homesteads with cattle and goats.

On choosing a target, they would surround the largest hut. The owner, rising to greet them, would be met by one Aathi elder holding a reddened *ndindi* stick high in the air. He would then place the tip of the stick within inches of the homeowner's eyes.

Having symbolically "bound" him by focusing his attention, the ritualist chanted the curse by which the homeowner would be struck if he failed to heed (i.e. feed) the group. Household heads who failed to provide an *aathi* band with goats, sheep, and cows of sufficient quality would awaken the next morning to find *nguchwa* (claw-sticks) planted at various point within the homestead—at gates, near goats, before a grain bin—where their gradual discovery could reinforce the fear of the curse.

As their flocks and herds increased, *aathi* bands began to dispense an alternate system of justice, different from those of either the *kiamas* or Crown. If one man believed another owed him two cows, he might simply join *aathi*, then ask its *kiama* ensure collection. If a ridgetop *kiama* made decisions that offended *aathi* elders, that group would circle the hut in which it met, marking their presence with *ndindi* sticks, liquid goat feces, and collectively chanted curses.

"U-u-u-u wikiri, twengwa wikiri, twengwana wikiri. U-u-u-u."
(o-o-o-o. Woe to you. If we lose, woe to you. If we win, woe to you.)

Kiama elders, listening inside, knew well that the same group could visit them each individually, extorting as much livestock as it wished. It was easier to submit collectively to *aathi* wishes.

Aathi vs. England

By 1928, both Lamb and Hopkins were thoroughly alarmed. Their first attempts to investigate what they saw to be secret societies were restricted to interrogating their interpreters, chiefs, headmen, and mission Christians. These were all young men, none likely to have even learned tribal secrets, much less reveal them to the conquerors. Nonetheless, weeks of intense inquiry convinced both men that members of their own colonial administration were being forced, through their own fear of supernatural curses, to join one (or more) of the societies, taking "dreadful oaths" to oppose every aspect of the British/Christian conquest. Violation of such oaths, of course, would mean sickness and death.

The second stage of what became a relentless inquiry was to interrogate the oldest of Meru's many elders. Caught between their fears of the fringe groups and the administration, the elders resorted to what they called "secret speech." Meru military tradition had allowed warriors, if captured by enemies, to reply indirectly to their questions, using proverbs, allegories, syllogisms, and even riddles as devices to avoid revealing facts. They did the same with Lamb and Hopkins, speaking in parables, allegories, riddles, and rhymes to avoid providing specifics.

Weeks of these conversations deeply angered both district officers, dependent as they were upon the British conversational patterns of brevity, directness and factual accuracy. Both men decided that the elders, through fear of being cursed, were all deliberately following the goal of passively obstructing the Government.

"It is essential, to make the work of both Government Headmen and Tribunals possible...to break the power of these societies. The powers of the witchdoctors are enormous and each witchdoctor is a member of a secret society. This innovation will be checked."

The Anti-Witchdoctor Campaign

Lamb and Hopkins then launched what they privately referred to an anti-witchdoctor campaign. They began with a series of public proclamations, riding through nearly all of the chief's camps, proclaiming that every known witchcraft group was to immediately disband. None did.

However, one single elder came secretly to Lamb, to offer help. Lamb asked him to name the leading members of his region who practiced witchcraft. To Lamb's complete surprise, the man provided names. This individual then told Lamb that because he had broken his oath, he would be dead in three days. He proved correct. His body, when examined by a British physician, showed "no sign of death." He had simply stopped.

Lamb then reacted in fury, ordering the immediate arrest of every known practitioner of witchcraft in Meru. With complete disregard for the subtleties of cursing vs. curse removal vs. curse detection, etc., he enlisted every European in the district to help "sweep up the lot." Missionaries, doctors, carpenters and agricultural specialists joined in with enthusiasm. As a result, 62 alleged practitioners—from both the *kiamas* and fringe groups—were rounded up within a single day and deposited in Horne's log-cabin jail.

Every one of them was old, bewildered, and terribly frightened. Hopkins questioned them all as a single group, jammed tightly into a single small room. He first asked who among them practiced *urogi* (cursing). Every single one denied it, claiming to be healers and thus innocent of causing harm.

"To demonstrate your innocence," Hopkins thundered, "every one of you will lick each other's magic powders."

The "magic powders" were, in fact, informal collections of roots, leaves, herbs, animal fat, and wildlife body parts (hooves, hearts horns, etc.), that each man had collected over years within the forest. The objects were then ground to powder and stowed within a goatskin bag that the ritualist kept always with him. Tragically, the bags had been collected beforehand. When passed back, no one knew if the *mithega* (magic substances) inside were his or those of another man.

Hopkin then commanded them to "lick the magic powders" from the bag they held. Every old man panicked! Meru tradition had taught them all to believe that only their own medicines offered safety; those of all other practitioners were poison. They licked. Most sickened and collapsed. Although rushed to the British doctor, ten died.

The remaining 52 were put on trial, administered by a British judge. All were found guilty. All were sentenced to prison, where most died. The death certificates listed the causes of death as old age, illness, etc. Neither Lamb nor Hopkins was punished—or even accused.

The impact on the entire Meru population was staggering. Some may have welcomed the imprisonment of *kagita* and *aathi* members, but were thunderstruck by the loss of respected curse removers, curse detectors and their own universally admired *kiama* elders.

On a deeper level, they were terrified to learn that no one was now permitted to remove a curse—which meant no one could heal. Nor could one resolve any conflict whatsoever between enemies. It was like saying that no one could ever again practice either healing or law enforcement. Westerners, faced with the simultaneous imprisonment of our doctors, nurses, and police would have felt the same. Without healing, how could one live—and why would one want to? Beyond healing, removing the system traditionally used to resolve individual conflicts, ancestral anger, and natural calamities left them psychologically defenseless.

Chapter 15

The Golden Years

Hopkins' indirect killing of the ritualists drove the spirit of the Meru people to its lowest point in tribal history. The entire Meru community descended into lawlessness and apathy. Senior elders no longer moved much beyond their homesteads, sinking into millet-beer-fueled silence. When district officers demanded their cooperation, they sullenly, silently responded as little as they felt would be allowed. When the authorities moved on, they returned to drinking.

The former warriors were worse. All of them were drinking, in universal defiance of the tribal tradition that restricted beer consumption to ruling elders. All of them had abandoned the tribal traditions of morality, which reserved all *akenye* (unmarried women) for their father's generation, now known as both junior elders and (potential) family heads.

In contrast, the years of warriorhood had required total sexual abstinence. However, since they were no longer warriors, they pursued *akenye*. This, of course, brought them into vicious and often violent conflict with the prospective family heads. As one result, many ex-warriors took up a new form of raiding, seizing cattle from the family heads, driving the beasts into the forests, and devouring them all. The conflicts led to a virtual epidemic of recurrent and wide-spread brawling.

Whites Who Loved Africans

At this time, however, Meru received two consecutive district commissioners, who saw themselves as administrator-anthropologists. Simply put, each of these men came to love the Meru, first learning the language and then striving to comprehend the culture.

Rather than sit in offices issuing orders to subordinates, these men spent their time seeking out the acknowledged "wise men" among the elders in each ridgetop. They came bearing the gifts that younger men traditionally brought to elders when seeking wisdom. They sat long hours, as groups of senior elders taught them *kiama*, describing the ways things had always been done.

"As a boy, I ran and hid from each Muchunku because they frightened me. As a warrior, I hated them. As an elder, I saw them change from fearful monsters to likable friends."

The first real change, initiated by the Government, was the restoration of the "*agambe* system." *Agambe* were spokesmen. When faced with conflict, each *kiama* (or *njuri*) chose one of its members to serve as spokesman for the group. Thus, ideally, each group of elders would have selected a spokesman to speak for its members to the government.

The Government's first attempts to restore this system did not go well. Hopkins, now remembered as the first of the "good" White DCs, asked each *njuri* and many *kiamas* to each select a spokesman.

Gradually, he appointed all of those chosen to the lower posts in Government. To ensure their loyalty, he paid each a salary. Their job was to aid the Government chiefs, headmen, and district officers to implement official decisions.

The attempt miscarried. The men selected saw themselves as spokesmen for their own *kiamas* and *njuris*. By accepting pay, they would have become spokesmen for the government, merely carrying out its orders. On realizing this, no one took the pay and almost all resigned. Nonetheless, elders across the region took note that *this* district commissioner was no longer trying to destroy everything Meru. By learning the language, inquiring after the tribal past, and attempting to use some of the traditions, Hopkins began to inspire both respect and the beginnings of trust.

Restoring Njuri

Meru's next district Commissioner, H.E. Lambert, continued the process. A gifted linguist, he learned fluent KiMeru within a few months. After weeks of patient discussion with leading *njuri* elders in every region, he decided to restore the entire *njuri/kiama* system.

His first attempt, though capturing universal attention, failed completely. That first step was to publicly revoke the Colonial ban on both systems. He did this through an extended series of public proclamations in which he (or an assistant) moved from region to region and village to village publicly reassuring the elders that their regional *njuri* and local *kiamas* could now meet in peace.

No one believed him. Elders everywhere either suspected a government trap or proved too apathetic to assemble. Abandoning the proclamations, the DC then moved through the villages, publicly praising the *njuri/kiama* system, and requesting its aid in resolving new problems. He supplemented these requests with visits to the most respected elders in each location, each time bringing the traditional gifts.

Over time, many elders found themselves impressed, both by his seemingly magical ability to speak their language and his obvious respect for Meru ways. Eventually, *njuri* members responded to his coaxing and hesitantly began to meet in daylight at their traditional gathering places. The DC responded to these tentative gestures by providing the bulls that tradition required for every *njuri* feast. Gradually reassured as to his intentions, the entire system of *njuris* and *kiamas* returned—however fearfully—to public life, beginning once more to resolve social conflicts.

Warrior Lawlessness Curbed

Once the ruling elders had been reintegrated into public life, government attention turned to the drunkenness and brawling of the warriors. The first decision was to revive the ancient tradition of *ntuiko*, the region-wide series of ceremonies by which each age-set moved simultaneously into a higher status.

Thus, throughout Meru, the warrior age-set, having completed its share of the rituals, would move up and into the combined status of family heads/junior elders. Now free of military obligations, their next task in life was to court and marry the *akenye* (unmarried), and sire children.

Junior elders, after completing their portion of the ceremonies, would become senior elders. Now free of family obligations, tradition allowed them to visit, feast, and drink copious qualities of millet beer and honey wine. Their traditional obligation had been to collectively make the decisions that guided tribal life. However, since these were now monopolized by the colonialists, they effectively retired.

Senior elders did retire. As those men nearest to death, they were also closest to the ancestors. One might call them the "ancestral" elders, since constant contact with their fathers (the ancestors) inspired both awe and respect. Traditionally, the young were required to seek them out to learn both their human wisdom and that imparted to them by the *nkoma.*

Tradition required the *ntuiko* to take place in two major steps. First, the *ndinguri* (older boys) along each ridgetop would organize themselves into a warrior band. As more and more boys reached the accepted age, the band grew larger—and stronger. At the same time, the warriors—theoretically secure in their *gaaru*—were losing members. As they aged, they began to yearn for cattle, a wife, and sons. One by one they left warriorhood.

Inevitably, the younger boys would attack. The remaining warriors would defend themselves, but inevitably—as tradition required—they would be physically expelled from the war-barrack and from warriorhood. It was their time to become junior elders and heads of families.

Only then could the existing junior elders act. Tradition required them to approach the senior elders, bearing large numbers of livestock and large quantities of beer. Negotiations might take considerable time. Tradition required, however, that agreement be reached. The juniors would become senior elders. The senior elders, now held sacred, would retire.

On learning of these traditions, the DC inquired repeatedly why the required shifts in status had not yet taken place. The elder's reply, repeated on ridgetop after ridgetop, was that locust invasions had destroyed the millet. With no millet, there could be no brewing of millet beer. With no beer, the senior elders would have nothing with which to bless the incoming juniors. Without the blessings, the watching ancestors would refuse to approve the entire transfer of authority. "The only solution," the DC was told, was "to wait another season—while hoping the locusts did not reappear—for new millet to grow. If none grew, they would wait another season."

The explanation was perfectly logical to every Meru. The DC disagreed. Importing millet from everywhere in Central Kenya, he moved from ridgetop to ridgetop, coaxing, explaining, and finally commanding that beer be brewed.

The transfer of power between junior and senior elders was thus swiftly completed. The warriors, no longer warriors, settled into their new roles as family heads. The endless brawls between that group and the former Junior elders over the unmarried women came to an end.

To a degree, Meru society was at peace. The former warriors were contented, with new wives and impending children. A fragile alliance between the colonial administration and the elders had come to life. The indigenous authorities had now resumed their work of resolving conflicts. To the DCs it must have felt like the dawn of a golden age.

If so, it was brief, the relative contentment of the elders did not include the young. In years to come, *ndinguri* school boys, influenced by a rising spirit of revolt among neighboring Gikuyu, would abandon both the churches and mission schools. No longer willing to obey any White, they would form independent schools and independent churches—using both the pulpits and the schoolrooms, to teach one another to strive for total freedom.

Chapter 16

Epilogue: Muchunku, There are More Stories to Hear

"Muchunku, why are you sleeping? There are more stories for you to hear."

The voice was that of Gituuru Gikama but it seemed be part of my dream. I had, in fact, been sleeping. Gituuru had spoken for hours, drawing often-fascinating word-pictures of the distant Meru past. As he did so, I had scrambled like a rabbit to keep up with him, laboriously writing down his words, trying to record his thinking, rather than reshaping it to fit my own ideas. Finally, it had become too much. As he rumbled on, with the words flowing out of his mind like sparks, I had quietly gone to sleep, note book on my lap, pen in my hand, glasses still on my nose.

"You are old, Muchunku," he said, not unkindly, after I was fully awake. "Elders must sleep. But there are many more stories for you to hear. When you wake, I will tell you first of what we Meru remember as 'good years.'"

Meru Independent Schools

One story will concern those Meru students who left their White-led Christian schools for African-led independent ones. Throughout the 1920s schooling was an educational monopoly, provided by White missionaries in alliance with the Colonial Government. The missionaries taught biblical

Christianity, but emphasized obedience to (White) authority, as one part of the subordinate role as the Children of Christ. Government officers believed that African education should be limited. As one colonial director of education expressed it:

"African brain capacity is inferior to (that of) the whites, hence the uselessness of higher (levels of) education for them."

Up to 1929, Africans were limited to "industrial education," which usually meant farming and crafts. Students alternated between classes and workshops. Never, however, were they introduced to new farming methods or the profit possibilities of new crops, such as coffee. The stated goal was to train children to grow up to work as labor for the Europeans.

African independent churches and then schools first emerged in Gikuyu. Those who founded the independent institutions simply launched "safe zones" where they could say and do and learn what they wanted—completely free from White influence.

Like their Gikuyu neighbors, Meru independent schools began by teaching English from the moment students entered. From there, many introduced mathematics and then sciences. Students grew school gardens, both to supply food and learn agriculture. A primary emphasis, however, was on what today might be called politics, within which adult Africans taught students about their tribal past, colonial present, settler racism, and African pride.

WWII: Meru in Combat

A second story will concern those Meru who entered global combat. WWII interrupted the Meru attempts to establish independent schools, as it did everything else. A military draft was launched across Kenya, and 98,240 Africans, including Meru, were inducted into British military service. They enlisted as *askaris*, a Swahili term that carries the image of an armed policeman (or soldier), ready to protect his land against its enemies.

The image was false. Kenyan African troops were shipped, alongside their White Kenyan counterparts, to fight against Italian troops in Northern Kenya, Somalia, and Ethiopia. Thereafter, British/Kenyan units were shipped to Burma to fight the Japanese. However, White troops in every Kenyan unit objected to their African soldier-comrades receiving guns.

Their first fear, however irrational, was that the Africans, once armed, would shoot the Whites. Their second objection, perhaps more logical, was that once having mastered both weapons and tactics, Africans would bring this knowledge back to Kenya to use in their fight for freedom. All Africans, they insisted, could contribute most to the war effort by loading and unloading goods, just as they had at home.

African soldiers were uniformly outraged. They had entered the British Army as *askaris*, not laborers. Their initial reaction was to "borrow" English weapons for short periods, then quietly return them. In those brief intervals, they taught one another to strip weapons, assemble them, aim, fire, use bayonets, and every other tactic possible. Later in the war, as White Kenyan casualties mounted, many African soldiers did see front-line service. As one Kenya veteran later put it:

"We (Africans) were told we were fighting for "our" country...and would be rewarded for the sacrifice we made. The life I returned to was exactly like the one I left: No land. No job. No dignity."

Meru in Mau Mau

"The final story, Muchunku, will tell of those among our people wo joined Mau Mau, to throw the British off our land forever."

Mau Mau was a Gikuyu rebellion, launched to retake the vast amounts of land that Whites had seized, while those Gikuyu living on it were forced to work for them as semi-slaves. The Meru, however, were not only neighbors to the Gikuyu, but thought of them as "cousins." Thus, when Gikuyu rebelled many young, idealistic Meru gladly joined, particularly the war-trained WWII veterans.

Every African faced the same demoralizing conditions on return to Kenya from the war. The promised "reward for sacrifices made" was a single small cash payment. Worse, Gikuyu ex-soldiers learned that Whites had seized still more thousands of hectares of their land and that they—the veterans—were expected to labor on the White *shambas* (farms) they had created, or risk arrest. They also met other Gikuyu, who had been forced out—in thousands—of the newly appropriated White areas. These fled to Nairobi. The educated refugees found low-level government jobs. The less educated, finding nothing, drifted into slums.

In despair, many slum dwellers formed associations through which to protest. When these failed, they began to flee into the dense, wet forests of the Aberdare Mountains and Mt. Kenya. Known as Mau Mau, they formed forest gangs, then began to attack White *shambas.*

Inspired by the dream of expelling all Whites forever, many Meru left both the independent schools and churches to flee into the Imenti, Igoji, Mwimbe, and Muthambe sections of the Mt. Kenya forest. Their first problem was to deal with the unrelenting wet cold.

"The rains stopped almost never and the cold, never, never. We only knew that we were still alive because we were always cold and wet."

Soon, every fighter dressed himself in monkey and antelope skins. Notwithstanding, the nights were not just cold and wet but dark, as neither moonlight nor stars could pierce the tree cover. Sandals were forbidden. They left tracks. If a fighter saw a sandal track, it meant someone was pursuing.

At sunrise, every fighter rose and prayed to the Meru God. Their prayers went up to Murungu, the traditional God of all Meru-speaking peoples, who lived on the peak of Mt. Kenya. Every man who voiced a prayer knew that he listened.

To move through the forest, the fighters followed elephant tracks. To eat, they hunted buffalos, wild honey, and such smaller game as they could spot and shoot within the undergrowth. To survive, however, they needed beans, yams, and millet. Sporadically, these were brought up the mountain by their wives. Otherwise, they could be had only by raiding the Meru *shambas* on the forest fringe—and these were defended.

Gikuyu Home Guard

The Colonial Government responded to the revolt by recruiting, training, and arming an ever-expanding Gikuyu paramilitary force, including 21,00 tribal police, 25,000 "Home Guards" (as the British named them) and 10,000 soldiers. This far outnumbered the the estimated 1500 Mau Mau fighters in the forests. The officers were Kenyan Whites, either Government district officers or Gikuyu-speaking settlers. Every Home Guard was armed—either with rifle or shotgun—and given a uniform.

The Home Guards proved uniformly effective. Most simply guarded the fortified villages into which Whites had swept those Gikuyu nearest the forest. Others, however, made constant sweeps through potential Mau Mau areas, causing considerable havoc.

"They (home guards) were always coming and we were always running."

The Meru Mau Mau, however, faced a unique and quite unexpected problem. Once they had established their bands, adjusted to the forest, secured adequate food and armed their fighters—there was nothing for them to do. Well-armed bands in Gikuyu areas could descend from the forest to strike

White *shambas*, killing livestock, burning crops, wrecking homes, and either terrorizing or killing the settlers.

The Meru fighters could do none of these things. Meru had no White settlers whatsoever. Those very few Whites residing in the Meru region were either colonial officers (too well defended to attack) or missionaries (too widely beloved to attack). In consequence, virtually all of the fighters' military efforts were directed against units of the Home Guards— or in evading efforts of the Home Guards to kill or capture them. The original purpose of flight into the forest simply slipped away.

Eventually, many of the fighters were captured. They were funneled into what the British called "the pipeline." The concept was originally conceived of as a forced rehabilitation. To the British, Mau Mau was to be treated as a form of insanity. In theory, captured fighters were to be moved along within a network of concentration camps. Within these, they were to be re-educated, and retaught farming, carpentry, and a return to British morality.

In fact, the various camps became nothing more than torture centers, where men and women alike were savaged until they had first confessed to having taken Mau Mau oaths, then renounced them. They would then be moved through a further series of camps, each less punitive than the last, until eventually released. They were then expected to take up low-paid employment in the service of Whites. Eventually, this was the fate of nearly every Meru forest fighter.

Finally, our Uhuru

Mau Mau lost its battle but won its war. The British had spent 55 million pounds to surpress the revolt, all in order to protect fewer than 60,000 Kenyan Whites. Many in Parliament felt that the rebellion would recur, expand, and go on forever. A few reforms were instituted: Kenyans (primarily Gikuyu) were allowed to own land and grow coffee. But the mutual hostility between Black and White remained the central facet of Kenya existence, until it became independent in 1963.

Muthungu, are You Listening?

There are so many more stories to tell. Once our country gained uhuru (freedom), Kenya's problems were many. I will tell you one story of the Somali shifta, increasingly well-armed bandits who have raided across Kenya's northern border from the first day of our uhuru to today.

I will tell you the story of Jomo Kenyatta, Kenya's first President and Mama Ngina, his wife and first lady; oh, I will tell you what they did both for Kenya and to it.

"I will tell you a war-story, about the war to either save or kill our animals, and the unending battles between those who argued that Africa was for Africans, not wild animals and those who wished to save every animal, even if Africans starved.

"For our Meru, however, uhuru meant changes that seemed small but ran deep. It meant the end of racist traditions, in which every word

of every White must be obeyed. It meant the end of Meru men being hailed by Whites as "Boy," in front of their own children. It meant that our Meru could work where they wanted and were no longer forced to work for Whites, who paid them almost nothing. At the deepest level, it meant that every Meru—every Kenyan—was now free to live his or her life as he or she preferred. What a wonderful gift is that to pass on to one's children?

"Sleep now, muthungu. When you wake, I will tell more. I will tell you the stories of our splendid Meru people until you die."

Life Stages of Meru Males

Age	Life stage/Meru term	Termination
0–7	Infant child / *Kiiji*	Appearance of second teeth
7–15+	Uncircumcised boy / *Mwiji*	Puberty
15–18+	Elder boy (candidate for circumcision) / *Ndinguri*–uncircumcised, *Ntaane*–circumcised	Circumcision
18–29+	Warrior (circumcised) / *Muthaka*	Marriage
29–40+	Family head (apprentice elder) / *Muruau*	Entry of first son into warriorhood
40–51+	Ruling elder / *Mzee*	Subsequent transfer
51–62+	Ritual elder (retired) / *Mzee*	Subsequent transfer
62+	The aged / *Mzee*	Death

Glossary

Aathi	Hunters
Aga	Curse removers (plural)
Agambe	Spokesmen
Akenye	Unmarried women
Aringia	Curse detectors (plural)
Arogi	Cursers (plural)
Aroria	Prophets, predictors of the future
Askari	police or soldiers
Aturi	Ironsmiths
Authi	Battle vows
Bunduki	Gun
chiti	Chit, pass
Gaaru	Warrior barrack
Gichiaro	Blood brotherhood / military alliance
Kachunku	Small Whites (derogatory, an insult)
Kagita	One sect of the "stomach kiamas"
Kallai	Curse using the carcass of a gazelle
Kangangi	"Little Walker," nickname for Edward B. Horne
Karambeta,	Half-flute, half-horn
Kiama	Elders' council
KiMeru	Meru language
Kiramana	One of the Meru age-sets
Kivunja	"The Destroyer," a District Commissioner
Mau Mau	Name of the Gikuyu rebels
Mbwa	Island, origin of the Meru
Miriti	One of the Meru age-sets
Mithega	Magic substances used by witchdoctors
Muga	Curse remover (singular)

Mugiro	Curse or spell
Murogi	Spell caster, curser
Muchunku	White man
Mugwe	Transmitter of ancestral blessings
Mumeru	Meru male
Muringia	Curse detector (singular)
Murungi	One of the Meru age-sets
Muthaka	Warrior
Mwiji	"Small boy," a deadly insult
Ndindi	Firesticks
Ndinguri	Older boys between 11–15
Ngweko/Nguiko	Leather "pubic apron" worn by women
Nguo Ntune	"Red Clothes," early invaders of Mbwa
Njuri Nceki	Ruling council of Meru elders
Nkima	"Skull," ritual magic used to guard a camp
Nkoma	Ancestral spirits
Nthaka	Warriors (plural)
Ntuiko	Ceremony for those moving to another age-set
Panga	Bush knife (short sword)
Shambas	European-owned farms
Shifta	Somali bandits from Northern Kenya
Simi	Short sword
Uga	Curse removal
Uhuru	Freedom
Uringia	Curse detection
Urogi	Cursing, causing a victim to sicken

Made in the USA
Middletown, DE
02 June 2023

31683316R00099